Badass Sisterhood

Roots and Wings

Badass Sisterhood
Roots and Wings

Badass Sisterhood Press

Copyright

All rights reserved. No part of this publication may be reproduced, distributed, or transmitted in any form or by any means, including photocopying, recording, or other electronic or mechanical methods, without the prior written permission of the publisher, except in the case of brief quotations embodied in critical reviews and certain other noncommercial uses permitted by copyright law. For permission requests, contact each author].

Each author is the sole copyright owner of the Work and retains all rights to the Work except for those expressly granted to Badass Sisterhood Press in this Agreement. (To the extent a separate copyright attaches to the Anthology as a collective work,) Badass Sisterhood Press is the copyright owner of any such copyright on the Anthology as a collective work.

First Edition
©2024 Laurie Riedman and Susan Walter, co-editors
Printed in the USA by Badass Sisterhood Press
Front Cover art by Wendy Coad
Photo Editing by Ellen Newman

ISBN 979-8-9901393-3-6

Every day is a journey and the journey itself is home. -Matsuo Bashō

Home is where our story begins....

Introduction

During the pandemic, Badass Sisterhood was formed in 2019 when women writers connected in an online writing community. The badass sisterhood has continued as these women continue writing and supporting one another.

This collection was inspired by the opposite concepts of roots and wings—the places that anchor us and the journeys that set us free. This anthology explores the intricate interplay of home and travel, capturing the duality of belonging and wandering.

As the world narrowed during the pandemic this past year, our imaginations took flight fueled by this online community of women writers – a sisterhood – where we found solace and strength in each other.

Badass Sisterhood: Roots and Wings is our collective exploration of what it means to be grounded and free, tethered and untethered, finding ourselves between staying and going.

This collection celebrates our collective voices, reflecting the duality of roots and wings.

Welcome, and we hope you enjoy our musings.

Laurie Riedman & Susan Walter
Badass Sisters and co-editors

Table of Contents

ROOTS

The Tour	1
Ariadne Horstman	
The Mystery of Where and When	27
Ellen Newman	
Home in Me	35
Sandra Holy	
Malagueña	41
Jackie Alcalde Marr	
She Stayed: A Chronicle of Enduring Friendship	57
T-Ann Pierce	
The Paradox of Progress	73
Amber Field	
Welcome Home	81
Laurie Riedman	
He Chews His Water	93
Susan Walter	
Cutting Flowers in My Mother's Garden	101
Katherine Cartwright	
How to Be an Artist...Where it Began	129
Wendy Coad	

WINGS

Ethiopia 2018, Quilts for Kids, and the Beggar Lady   **137**
    Terri Tomoff
Butterfly Wisdom   **145**
    Katharina Hren
Dust Sandwiches   **153**
    Amber Field
Spanish Family Trip   **161**
    Maggie Ford Croushore
Meeting Mother India   **193**
    Laurie Riedman
Musings from 36,000 Feet   **205**
    Ellen Newman
Patria or Homeland   **211**
    Jackie Alcalde Marr

Author Biographies   **213**
Acknowledgements   **244**

# ROOTS

The Tour

This is an excerpt from a longer project in progress, entitled potentially High and Dry in Hyderabad.

Ariadne Horstman

"Time for the tour." Gagan called as Arabella surveyed the apartment. Suitcases, half open, lay about, their contents scattered on the floor.

"Let's meet the other faculty and check out the place."

The institution was fashioned after Arab architecture, a nod to Hyderabad's ancient culture of Nizams and palaces. Blocks of sand-colored stone rose up in clean lines to form buildings designed to blend in with the Muslim-influenced city and withstand intense heat. A circular road ran round the main building, flanked by acres of lawn and scrawny young trees that demonstrated the newness of the place. Clearly landscaping a boulder-strewn plateau was not easy.

As they walked along with Sanjay, the head of department who had hired Gagan, they commented on the cool and pleasant weather that morning.

"Enjoy it while you can!" laughed the first professor they met. "This is winter. Temperatures will soon be in hundreds, till rainy season."

Coming from temperate Northern California, Arabella wondered how she would manage in the heat they were talking about. Anxiety filled her as she contemplated the coming spring. Gagan had grown up in Rajasthan and was used to this kind of climate. Like many things in their relationship, he had no qualms over issues that caused her to lose sleep at night. The kids lived for the moment and did not give a hoot about temperatures. They ran jumping and bounding, exploring with unlimited energy. She did not share their excitement and found it hard to handle in her frazzled state.

They met more staff and spouses on their tour, who all complained of the daily existence: poor medical care, help impossible to keep or manage, low-quality schools, cooks and drivers running amok.

"Just buy a dishwasher, for god's sake, the maids here are terrible." Snorted one man who was tall and built like a stretched-out Winnie the Pooh. He towered above them, his soft middle area swaying dangerously about, like a skyscraper in the wind that had not been well anchored.

"Dishwasher, Dryer, you are set. No hired help, no trouble."

"And I am driving now!" proudly stated a generously proportioned lady that must have been his wife. "Imagine! Driving in India! Death defying act!" She laughed with a cackle. "But having a driver? So much trouble…." She threw up her hands to express the fact.

Most of the teaching staff were Indians who had done a stint or two on other continents, acquiring degrees at prestigious foreign universities. They had come back nostalgic and curious, like Gagan, wanting to see how life might be as a professor at a fancy business school in their country of origin.

"Let's go to my office", proposed Sanjay, cutting the tour short, as he steered them to the main building. Perhaps he noticed they were not getting the kind of intro he had foreseen, thought Arabella, and wanted to reassure them. A personable man, she hoped he would be their guide as they transitioned to this new life. Perhaps his wife would be her first friend.

His office was large with a shiny marble floor that seemed typical of the place. They sat down, relaxing, as Sanjay had shown them where it was safe to leave the kids -- reading books in the light filled atrium library.

"I've just gotten an offer" he stated casually, looking out the window over the lawns, snapping her back to reality and eradicating any ease she had begun to feel. "I'll be leaving soon for a post at the University of Michigan." He paused to gage the response.

Her husband did not react, something he excelled at, as Arabella absorbed the sudden reversal. What did that mean if the person who had hired Gagan was leaving already?

"Of course, I will get you situated." He rushed to reassure them, clearing his throat. "We're inviting you to Christmas lunch. At our home."

She took in the handsome building they sat in with its deep leather chairs and shook off the thought things might be amiss. She was a world traveler. She had been to India many times and lived in France. She could do this.

It had taken her time to get settled in Paris and become fluent in French, but she had been quickly accepted and swept up into a group of friends. Known as "L'Americaine", she went to people's country houses at the weekend, and they invited each other to incessant dinner parties to stave off possible discontent with the grey damp weather. Movies, intense intellectual discussions in cafes, and outings to ride horses in the forests outside the city defined her days. It had been a lovely way to pass her twenties. She just had to find her tribe in Hyderabad...

New Housing

Returning to the apartment, they applied themselves with difficulty, due to the limited sleep they'd had, to necessary tasks like signing up for internet, acquiring cellphones and cooking gas.

"Mommy, the bathroom is flooding!"

Arabella rushed to find her son confronted by an overflowing toilet. Unsure what to do, she was rescued by a knock at the front door. Opening it revealed a fellow with tattered sandals.

"Pest control" he uttered, looking at the floor. Gagan arrived beside her and launched into Hindi to explain how the house was full of mosquitoes, they needed better window coverings, and why had it taken him so long to show up?

"Thank god he speaks the language," she thought.

"Sir." he said haltingly. "No Hindi. Telegu only."

"Oh crap." He let out a long breath of frustration from dealing with such menial tasks. He had come to be a professor, and he was handling pest control?

"But it's like Hindi, right? You understand it?" His wife said hopefully.

"Not at all, totally different language. "

"Well, can you call a plumber? The bathroom is flooding."

"You call! There's the phone, call facilities, they speak English."

He thrust a photocopied list of numbers into her hand as he gesticulated at the man, trying to describe mosquitos in the air.

It became rapidly apparent that much of daily life took place in the local language. She knew India had many regional languages but had no idea people would *only* speak those, especially at the Hindu School of Business campus, which she had been led to believe was a cosmopolitan place.

The apartment was so new, the paint was hardly dry. It appeared to have been thrown together in a hurry, perhaps finished the day before. Spackle and grout were smeared over tiles, kitchen appliances, and windows. Gaps showed around doors. Much of the brand-new furniture provided was flecked with paint.

The first floor of the building was theirs with numerous doors leading to the outside, which made Arabella nervous. She didn't like so many points of entry and the locks were **befuddling**. The quantity of keys handed over made her feel like a jailer and she had no idea which one opened what except that the second key to the left on the ring opened the front door. She worried she might forget to lock all the entrances, and someone might get in. Then again, if there were a fire, they might be trapped inside – what if everything was locked and she couldn't find the keys? With bars on all the windows, how would they get out?

As soon as they got working internet, she emailed HSB's administrative office asking them to provide the escape plan in case of emergencies.

"We don't have fires, Madam," replied the fellow who called back on the house phone. "The buildings are stone."

Meanwhile, the doorbell wouldn't stop ringing.

"Hello Madam, I am here to check phone".

"We are housekeeping boys. Wash floors, sweep."

"Facilities for repairing plumbing-- toilet not functioning?"

"Milkman. Wanting milk daily?"

People kept coming even though little was happening. Many seemed to have their own keys and walked right in. Everyone knew the first sentence to say in English

7

but after that it was a gamble as to which language they might speak. Her head swam with sensory overload.

Pizza Hut

The first trip off campus was to Pizza Hut, where their son might eat. Breakfast was good at the cafeteria but for the rest of the day, the only thing on offer was Indian Food and Rahil preferred to go hungry rather than try a cuisine his 7-year-old palate found to be highly offensive.

Having secured a car and driver, they left the front gates of the spacious and peaceful gated community and discovered most of Hyderabad to be a loud, active construction site with bulldozers and dynamite teams operating 24/7. There appeared to be a great hurry to build out the city.

Arabella had expected a *Bangalore Bis*, a carbon copy of the sophisticated, mature metropolis hosting high-tech companies and their workers with ample infrastructure.

"Hyderabad is basically Bangalore, just in a different location" Gagan had told her confidently. Since she had seen and approved of Bangalore, which offered everything they needed from Western style supermarkets and department stores to international restaurant chains to feed their son, she'd seen no reason to vet Hyderabad before agreeing to live there.

Caveat Emptor. Gagan had not come to Hyderabad either, accepting the job straight off the bat. But he was not bothered by the state of the city. It was close enough to home and he was content to be back in India.

They drank in the views from the moving car. Tall towers emerged from the earth at a breakneck pace. Giant Highways extended for one mile, then stopped abruptly with a construction crew laboring feverishly at the edge (or as feverishly as construction crews could labor in the hot midday sun).

They drove past Microsoft, Amazon, Deloitte and more western companies as the construction continued. And destruction-- of nature.

Settlements of blue plastic tents lined the roads with women outside cooking on open fires. Everywhere was mud, dirt, and piles of raw materials like rocks. And more dirt. This part of the city was in the full birthing stage --terrifying, raw and wondrous.

Forty-Five minutes away in Madhapur, Pizza Hut welcomed them in, fed them and offered respite. Never were they happier to see a chain restaurant!

The Household

Back at the campus, Arabella worked on getting the washing machine to run. The microwave was incomprehensible except for one button that had a picture of a teacup on it and ran 1 minute and 36 seconds. She washed the few dishes on hand, which were constantly dirty, hunched over a single spout that produced a thin stream of tepid water. The kitchen sink was positioned at a height too low for her as a tall woman, probably designed for the typical stature of local ladies.

Gagan shared good news as he left for the office, "I found someone who agreed to work 3 hours a day. Don't worry, help is coming." His wife glared at him.

Ten minutes later the woman showed up at the door.

"Needing talking Sir."

"I can help" said Arabella sweetly, hoping to show her what a kind employer she would be.

"You can do dishes? Laundry?"

The woman grunted and came in to stand sullenly by the door. "Sir" she repeated.

"Sir is in office. How are you doing today?"

She waited a few minutes while Ara tried vainly to telephone Gagan and then swept out with her sari swishing behind her.

"Telling sir one hour only" She called over her shoulder imperiously as she left.

"One hour is perfect, great! See you tomorrow!"

But she was never seen again. Sir was required for many transactions but was little available. Arabella was not considered a suitable interlocuter. She did not speak Hindi, let alone Telegu and was a firangi, foreigner. No one wanted to talk to the imposing looking white lady.

It was Christmas break and there was no school. Her offspring ran her ragged with little to entertain them. It had not been easy for her to raise children in any circumstances, but she had constructed a world in Los Altos that functioned.

It had not occurred to her prior to having children that her own traumatic upbringing might make it difficult to provide the kind of childhood she wanted to offer. She vowed to raise her kids better; to provide regular meals, consistent bedtimes and financial stability. She hadn't counted on her fragility in the face of screaming tantrums and endless days of tedium. She had made it bearable only through a careful balance of community and family support, along with paid childcare. All of which had suddenly disappeared.

"You can be going to Qmart if you want the Western foods," Said a neighbor. Arabella requested a car from the campus front desk.

"Yes, Madam, 10 minutes car arriving."

She got the kids ready, and they went out on the sidewalk to wait. Leela found some flowers to pick and Rahil, bored, snuck up from behind and pulled her hair. "Mommy!" shrieked her daughter and thus Forty-five minutes of similar behavior ensued while they waited for the car. Eventually a man pulled up and asked if she was Arabhi.

"No."

"Well, probably. That's it, yes," she said, imagining it could be a mispronunciation. If it was not, she needed the car and had better take it. The sun was getting higher, and she had begun to sweat, not daring to go back inside, lest they miss the driver's arrival. Once in the small vehicle, having established there were no seat belts, to her consternation, they started towards the town.

"Sir, can you please put on the air conditioning?" It was decidedly baking as the heat of the day filled the car.

"No AC."

"I'm hot." complained Rahil, "How far is it?"

"Sir, how long will it take?"

"Jubilee Hills? Forty-five. Taking time. Many traffics."

"You're stupid" Said Rahil to Leela.

"Am not!" She replied.

"What's 85 plus 34?" he questioned, determined to prove his point. Not sure what to respond, she used the most logical tactic available to her, and whacked him. Arabella struggled to separate the children who lunged across the back seat with no seat belts to restrain them. As they neared the city, traffic increased, and the honking was incessant. She wanted to whack both the children herself. If only they would shut up!

Finally, they reached the store and entered a cool air-conditioned mecca of familiar products. "Cheerios!" Cried the kids. They filled the cart with cheeses and butter from France, cereal from the US, and fruits they recognized, like apples, from Kashmir. They were ecstatic to find their favorite foods.

Ara was presented with a bill at checkout that she had not thought possible in an Indian Supermarket. *I'll have to pay attention next time, she thought— 10$ for a box of cheerios?* Laden with supplies and dreaming of eating a comfort food lunch of toasted cheese sandwiches, they left and searched the parking lot for the driver. Arabella cast her eyes over rows of unfamiliar cars. Drivers stood in a group chatting.

"Hello," she called out.

"I'm looking for our driver."

Silence fell upon the group as all eyes turned in her direction.

"Which driver looking?"

"Uh, Noori travels car?"

They conferred amongst themselves.

"Tea break."

"Tea break?"

"Gone for Chai. Just coming."

She stood with the kids in a corner of the lot as they jumped around, swatting each other while cars raced in and out, perilously close.

"Be careful!"

"Stay here!" Her voice rose.

"Stop running! It's dangerous! I'm going to take away your screen time."

"There will be a consequence!"

Where was the driver? How could she control the kids with her hands full of groceries? What if he never came back? What if the butter melted and went bad in the heat? She had no idea who he was or how to get in touch with him.

At last, he returned, and the siblings carried their grievances into the car. It was harder to endure them tussling in a small, enclosed space, although there was less chance for injury now they were out of the parking lot. She intensely missed her minivan where they could be strapped into seats far from each other, out of hitting range and soothed with videos she could switch on to divert them. Even Baby Beluga cassette tapes would have been a help. She struggled to keep her temper in check as the kids battled all the way home.

Schools

The driver located the school on a side street of Jubilee Hills. It was a rich neighborhood and the houses they passed were palatial mansions, done up in both good and bad taste, lining the leafy green avenues. Some seemed modeled on the American White House, with columns and size to match. Ara marveled at the big homes. She had not seen the likes of these on previous Indian travels aside from grand hotels that were renovated Palaces.

Leaving the car, they faced a large building of uncertain color, heritage or style. The street was dusty, standing out from the surrounding fancy neighborhood. The school entrance was forlorn and the children playing on the front steps in a heap of chaos looked unkempt. Ara began to have an uncomfortable feeling in her stomach as she realized they had prepaid thousands of dollars for the school, sight unseen.

They found the office and a cheerful person showed them around the sleepy old structure. The steps were stone and the balustrades marble, but the building could not shake off centuries of grime that coated the place inside and out. The playground was surfaced in hardpacked dirt with a rusted-out swing set that exposed sharp metal edges. Ever on the lookout for safety, Ara made mental notes on potential dangers. Rahil, not a particularly well-turned-out child, due to his mother's lack of attention to his wardrobe and stronger focus on getting the kids dressed, rather than dressed smartly, was in an uncharacteristically clean outfit of clothes that stood out in the rag tag bunch of students. He looked around with displeasure. "It's dirty" he said disdainfully. Even Gagan, less discerning in the safety and hygiene area, seemed dubious.

There was more to the tour but after seeing the playground, it was over for Arabella. "The kids can't go here!" she whispered to Gagan, poking him. "It looks dangerous! Did you see the swing set?"

Dutifully they had looked up the schools while in the US, from a list provided to them, reviewing each one on the internet, trying to decipher what they might actually be like. They nixed the international school due to cost. Though the professor's salary at HSB was good by local Standards, it was not sufficient to support two children at a swanky place intended for high-flying expat executive offspring.

Private Indian schools displayed pictures of straight lines of children with long, tight braids. They radiated academic excellence and strict discipline. Uniforms in order, shoes shined, smiles applied. The couple shook their heads and agreed, that approach would not work. Their son attended an alternative school with no grades, homework or lines of any kind, straight or otherwise.

The most interesting choice seemed to be the Doldorf, promising holistic education and affordable pricing. Ara had long dreamed of sending the kids to such a school in Silicon Valley--completely out of their price range— so she jumped at the chance to get a bargain on the kind of education she wanted for her offspring. They wired the down payment and signed up. As she stood inside that very school, far from the internet photos, she knew there was no way she could send her children there.

There was nothing to do but venture a visit to the *International School of the Deccan Plateau*. Arabella alighted onto a campus awash in clean, white structures with lush gardens and tall Palm Trees. Black and white marble floors were shined to a fault and squeaky clean. The person who showed them around was polite and the principal was German. Not a speck of dust dared show itself. She breathed out a sigh of relief. It seemed acceptable.

Seeing the cafeteria which served Western Food brought a smile to her face and a full-time onsite nurse allayed more fears. Knowing India was a place where one could come down with Malaria at any time, especially a thin child like her Rahil-- surely unable to resist local diseases-- having medical staff would be so comforting. She imagined how she would relax during the day, knowing her son was occupied and safe. It would be heaven. She closed her eyes imagining it, feeling the anxiety wash away.

Large play yards seemed comparatively clean, and the school boasted air conditioning. "It keeps the kids alert and healthy in the hot season." explained her guide.

"We'll sign him up", said Arabella firmly. She was not sure how they would pay for it, but she did not care.

Not finding the help she had heard so much about, she set herself to the task of housewifery. She washed dishes and scrubbed the kitchen spotless to keep away cockroaches. Laundry was hung out to dry al fresco. Every morning and evening, she made rounds of the many rooms to turn on and off plug-in mosquito empoisoning devices and check if they were full of the toxic liquid that powered them. She wondered what kinds of fumes they were sending out into the house, as she weighed that against the risks of mosquito borne infections.

She searched the apartment at dusk as the flying beasts started to come out, trying to figure out how they were getting in and where. She laid down on the floor to measure the gaps under the large glass doors in the living room and every day found a new opening through which Mosquitos flowed in liberally at night.

"Facilities? Please send someone. I found another place to close up."

They had been told not to bring Malaria tablets as they couldn't be taken for two years straight. Anyway, Dengue fever was more dangerous and there was no pill for that. But she couldn't stop the insects from getting in and they were covered with bites, each one potentially leading to a fatal tropical disease in Arabella's eyes.

"What's the worry?" Said Gagan. "I had malaria twice. Yellow fever once. Typhoid. Even Cholera. Look at me! I'm fine."

She rolled her eyes. Fine for him, but their children were American and had no constitution for such things.

She went to the campus park to gather intelligence. Hanging out while the kids played was the best way to connect with other moms and collect information.

"Leave the ceiling fans on at night above the beds-- that keeps them away as you sleep" said one.

"Ahh, good idea."

She took notes.

"I use mosquito nets," said another.

"Where can I buy them?" She retorted. She was ready to drive anywhere to procure these. She would do what it took. Why hadn't she thought of this before?

"We brought them from the US."

She began to realize she had been hopelessly unprepared for their move. She had not imagined it would be so hard. She had lived in other countries and done just fine.

Burning inside with frustration, she recalled just a few weeks before, being happy in her beloved Los Altos, her days punctuated by naps, workouts at the gym with childcare, and friends dropping by for playdates. She had not wanted to come to India, but knew Gagan yearned for his country, and thought, how hard could it be? It would be a fun interlude.

Now, left on her own with the kids, she was losing it on a daily basis and no one was happy with her, least of all herself. She felt furious at her husband for duping her into coming to Hyderabad.

"Mommy, come sit by my door." Rahil called. He liked her to sit outside his bedroom while he fell asleep. When his eyes closed, her whole body relaxed -- it was a luxury to have time by herself without anticipating the next meltdown and her own inability to deal with it. But she was lonely with no friends and her husband out late.

She had imagined herself relaxing by a pool in India, wearing a large hat and Bollywood sunglasses and not lifting a finger, as her slender body bronzed (in her dreams she would tan instead of her own white skin turning angry red in the sun). She was sure she would become slim with full time childcare, waitstaff, custom prepared food and all day to spend at the gym. Flunkies would gather round, plying her with fresh fruit and cool drinks. "Madam? Can I polish your sunglasses? Can we select a lovely outfit for your dinner party tonight?"

She had prepared for that scenario, packing and shipping boxes of photos and empty albums she planned to work on in the ample free time she imagined lay ahead. Most pictures were still packed in the envelopes from the places that had developed the film. Now the whole business was going digital, leapfrogging albums, before she could even fill them up with paper copies. But she was not going to let those expensive Creative Memories scrapbooks go to waste. The darling and nemesis of every American Mom of the era, the brand was beloved by the women who somehow found time to compile elaborate photo books while also dressing well, turning out polite, clean children at parties and being "Nice" to everyone. The women who hated it were like Arabella; tired, dressed in comfortable clothes with unstyled hair and accompanied by bratty children talking back, attired in whatever they could find by themselves, usually hand me downs since she could not be bothered to go to chic shops in air-conditioned malls. She preferred to be out hiking or riding horses at every available moment of non-kid time. And she wanted her kids playing in parks and getting dirty rather than trailing behind her in stores. Designer clothes for kids were a waste of money anyway.

Still, she wanted those scrapbooks and dreamed of being "that kind of mom". She occasionally had worked on them late at night, on the odd chance she could not sleep. Usually, she passed out with the kids after exhausting days, and the clean white pages of her photo albums bore testimony to her inability to preserve memories for her family.

Gagan was still not home at 11pm but at a fancy hotel for some conference. It was dark and the large apartment echoed eerily. She was too scared to go in the laundry room to chuck in a load or even to sleep so she took up her journal.

"Dear Diary,

I've had multiple invitations to fancy dinners with Gagan since we got here at hotels, palaces and other elegant venues. I brought all the saris and jewels I received for my wedding, thinking I could finally wear them. But other faculty moms already told me they never go to anything since they have to take care of the kids. No one here trusts maids to babysit, especially at night but we don't even have a maid to not trust. Those fancy dinners that take place on the lawns with white tablecloths and flickering candles? The effect is beautiful, and I seethe with envy every time I walk past the servers setting up in the early evenings, dragging my burnt-out children home to dinner. Why am I not fitting in and finding a group of friends? In France I settled right in and never looked back. Shouldn't I, a citizen of the world, be able to do this? I've been to India so many times and love its beauty and exoticness, but living here is so hard!"

The Mystery of Where and When

Ellen Newman

Although I've lived in my house in San Francisco for more than 40 years, I don't actually think of San Francisco as home. It's hard to explain why I don't feel at home in this city loved by so many.

Maybe it's because I'm from Los Angeles, and the civic rivalry can be fierce. Or maybe it's because of the weather. San Francisco summers are cold and foggy, not bright and sunny. July can feel as gloomy as January, and Fogust is aptly named. It's hard to love a town that obliterates my favorite season.

But those are surface thoughts, excuses really. I've been meandering down a twisty path, pondering the concept of home since I've had the privilege of traveling to many parts of the world and discovering that for many people home is much more than the house one lives in.

My question about what home means started in Jojowar, a gritty, dusty Rajasthani farm town far from the romantic fantasies of Indian travel brochures and Bollywood movies. Cows, motorbikes and autorickshaws jostled for space in the market square with women in bright saris, men in colorful turbans and clusters of barefoot children. That's where I met Rao Maharaj Singh, owner of Rawla Jojawar, an 18th-century garrison fort, transformed like so many secondary royal properties into a boutique hotel.

"My seventh-generation grandpa, he built this house," Rao Singh told me. It was about 300 years back, before the British colonized India, that his ancestor was gifted the land for valor on the battlefield. A few days later, we stayed at the remote Ramathra Fort, also in Rajasthan. This time I was told that the family that owns the property can be traced 11 or 12 generations back.

We heard similar tales much closer to home in Santa Fe, New Mexico. On our first visit in 2021, our waiter at an elegant restaurant recounted stories about his family dating back to the Spanish conquest in the 1600s. With equal measures of pride and embarrassment, he told us how his forebear was part of the force that terrorized the Pueblo peoples. And in Taos, after we toured the historic Martinez hacienda, the greeter at the entrance told us how she and her sisters traveled to Spain to finish tracing the multigenerational history of their family. And of course, the people of the Taos Pueblo trace their lineage back more than a thousand years.

As the stories accumulated, I became conscious that I have no idea about my family history beyond my grandparents and one great-grandmother. Bubba Pesha, my mother's grandmother, was a legend, a Brooklyn Jewish midwife who helped birth Senator Jacob Javits and composer Leonard Bernstein.

Most of the rest of what I know about my grandparents is hearsay, tropes recited by my parents from their catalog of memories. "Everyone loved Grandpa Fred." Maybe so, but why? Fred was my maternal grandfather, but that's all I know. He died a couple of years before I was born. "You are named after Eva. She was the kindest person in the neighborhood. People always came to her with their troubles." Eva was my dad's mom. At least three girls were named for her.

The only grandparent I ever met was Fanny, Fred's widow. A heavy-set woman who spoke more Yiddish than English, she was a stern matriarch presiding over her Brooklyn family. At least that's how it looked to me at three, seven, ten and eleven years old when we visited New York from Los Angeles. I was the baby of six grandchildren, and probably not of much interest to her.

She was from a different world, 19th-century Central Europe. My aunts said she was from Austria, but Austria in those days encompassed most of Central Europe. Her story: she didn't like her stepfather, so she escaped to New York as a teen to live with an aunt. That must have taken a great deal of chutzpah, but it's not a story she told or a lesson she passed on to us.

My dad's parents were from Nesvizh, a town near Minsk, now in Belarus. Once upon a time it was part of Lithuania, followed by the Polish-Lithuanian Commonwealth, the Russian Empire, the Soviet Union, Poland, Nazi Germany and back to the USSR before it broke up. This is not a place to call home, a place to go back to in order to find one's roots. Those roots have been pulled out, eradicated for good. Ethnic cleansing happened. Luckily my grandparents left before the worst of it, settling in New York.

I tell people that Brooklyn is my "old country." The Brooklyn I visited as a kid was a strange, exotic place. My cousins lived in apartments, not houses. On my first visit, vegetable sellers and other peddlers hawked their wares from horse-drawn carts. The kosher butcher was half a block away, and my aunts could choose a live chicken for dinner that night.

One Friday when I was ten or eleven, just before evening my aunts and mom ushered me upstairs to peek into Grandma's room. A lace scarf over her gray hair, she was lighting Shabbat candles, barely whispering the blessing. Now, looking back, I wonder, why was she saying the blessing in her room, alone, instead of in the kitchen with the rest of the family. Passing down traditions didn't seem to be a priority. The immigrant generation left the places they were born for safety and opportunity—and found it in America. They were glad they left. And for them, that was that.

I'm clearly a transplant three times over. My grandparents moved to America at the end of the 19th century. My parents moved to California during the Great Depression. My husband and I moved to San Francisco for law school. And our son moved to the East Coast for college and stayed. Transplants all.

So where is home? Is it the place where I grew up? I always get a prickle of excitement when we drive over the ridge separating California's Central Valley from Los Angeles. The highway is wide—eight lanes—and fast. It curves as it drops steeply down into the San Fernando Valley. Almost home, my arms tingle, even though the house I grew up in is now someone else's home.

Or is home the place where I live now, where I raised my child, where I've been happy and sad, sick and well? Is home the place of roots and generational memory or the place that has Today written all over the lists, the chores, the cups of tea, the nibbles from the fridge, the dinner parties and the cocooning in front of the TV?

As I try to sort out the concept of home, I wonder: is home the Los Angeles house and neighborhood where I grew up or the Central European towns where my grandparents came from? Is home the taste of oft-repeated family recipes or the exotic flavors of the café down the street? Is it the setting for the stories of our ancestors or the safe nests we make for our children?

Maybe home is all these things, a mosaic of memories and longing, bits and pieces that make a life of meaning. Yes, there are missing pieces in my mosaic, mysteries that will never be solved. But the mystery, the absence, is part of my story. As I think about it further, I realize that it's also part of the American story. We are a land of people from other places, notoriously vagabond, following jobs and opportunities until we create that place called home for ourselves and our children.

HOME IN ME

Excerpted from, "The Singing Bird: A Memoir About the Hidden Story of My Life."

Sandra Holy

In the still, dark hours before dawn, I rose from my lover's bed. His black hair fell onto the pillow in smooth and unkempt waves. The angles of his face were softened by his surrender to sleep. Had he done harm to others? Did he intend harm? And, if so, was there something I should do about that?

I stood over him and watched the soft rise and fall of his chest as he slept; felt somehow reassured by the feel of him in this restful state. It wasn't enough to still me and I turned away, hoping to find calm in another room.

Luminous shades of moonlight bathed the walls as I trod quietly down his hallway. I turned into the living room, passed a full-length mirror: went another two steps, stopped. *"What was that?"*

I backtracked a few steps and peered into the mirror's inky depths. Stepping back to look at my reflection from a distance I saw, in that muted light, the form of a woman: tall, long-limbed; beautiful. Could that be me?

I proceeded toward the glass doors that fronted his balcony and gazed out. A pregnant moon filled the sky. I planted my unsteady feet into whatever grounding the carpet could offer; then sang to her. I offered her all of me: my broken parts, my naked body and the groundswell of some fathomless and timeless essence that flooded through me as if I were a conduit.

Quiet, clear notes arose from deep in the well of my soul. I let the moon's subtle light wash over me, hoping it would quell the relentless churn of my overactive mind. Even now, that mind sought answers through a ceaseless process of sorting, sifting and evaluating what had transpired in these past long hours.

All I wanted was to be washed: to have this whole business – all the fear, and all that was not me – washed off of me.

While one part of me sang, another part observed what was happening within me: watched patterns of fallen logic playing across my mind, like an infinite sequence of meaningless numbers running across a silent computer screen. I considered the possibility that my mind had broken.

This consideration soon became the backdrop to a greater event. I felt the moon's radiance suffuse my being, as if my body were no more than a sponge soaking up her light, and I a moth fluttering to the promise of her milky glow.

My body felt insubstantial and hollow, as if my skin was a flimsy encasement for the shaft of moonlight it contained and my body no more than a shell; a cylinder waiting to be filled.

As I stood there, the moon dressing my naked body with her waxen light, I may as well have been Eve, Pandora and the High Priestess, all rolled up in one.

I may as well have been, on that dramatic night, a heroine in one of the Mary Stewart novels that I'd raptly devoured in my teens.

For here I was, standing in my own mystery, enmeshed in the intrigues of a story that could very well be my end: romance dancing around me while danger pressed at my skin. And here I stood, yet to traipse or plod across the pages of my own unfinished story, however sweet or sordid its end might prove to be.

All the while, boggling questions continued to impose their weighty pull on my mind. Why had I understood what my lover told me, as if I already knew? Who was I: the non-descript woman that I'd believed myself to be until so recently; or this larger-than-life woman who seemed to be arising in me: a woman who appeared to understand all this grand, cosmic stuff with hardly more than the blink of an eye?

In the end it was music that lulled the questioner in me to sleep. Classical pieces that I'd heard as a child, on my mother's records. I now sang these, for what felt like an eon. When I ran out of known pieces to sing, a chant arose from within: my own song to the moon.

I sang my way, softly and determinedly, through the night. As if these songs were my protection: a shield between me and whatever dark force this man was linked to; a barrier through which that dark force could not reach me; because without question, every sense in my body warned – in this house – dark was all around.

I sang my notes as if they were the sounds of the very light protecting me: understood this to be so, without having known or imagined it before.

I offered my songs out to the moon, and back to myself: tendered them like offerings in some great duet, for my own comfort and solace; while my heart sought protection and my mind sought guidance from a source greater than myself, to help me make sense of what I could not comprehend. Guidance came, silent and wordless.

That is when the Mother-in-Moon was birthed, for me. On that night, under that moon, when all that I had believed about myself beforehand was erased – deleted – from my world of preconceived notions. From that night, the Moon became my Mother and I, Her servant: a priestess, in my own way.

That is when I discovered the sanctuary awaiting within: the night I found the home in me.

Malagueña

Jackie Alcalde Marr

I know she's not real. She is barely visible in the shadows of the sprawling oak, but I see her there beside the creek. She slides her hands across her temples, smoothing her hair and tucking a few loose strands back into the tight bun at the nape of her neck. She must be hot under that thick skirt and tight bodice, all black and buttoned up to her throat. She turns to look at me, her lips pulling into a smile. Well, it's *almost* a smile. It's too tight, too pained to share any joy with me.

The light shifts and she fades from view.

I'm standing on the small bridge where my favorite walking trail crosses a creek and bends to the left. The water in the creek curls around rocks and twists its way toward me, glistening white as it spills fast over roots and fallen logs. My eyes follow it upstream, searching between the barren branches at the water's edge. Searching for her. Then the breeze cools my cheek and lets the light in between the branches, and that's when she appears again - Bernarda, my great-grandmother.

Her eyes – so much like my own eyes – look downstream to me. Her eyes want to tell me of her life, of her fateful choices, of her sorrow, and of her joy.

But the shadows shift and take her from me again.

No one else is on the bridge this morning, leaving the sacred moments to me alone. In my ears, I hear Spanish guitar. The same high note hammers in between the others, a quick and syncopated rhythm. "Malagueña." It's my favorite Spanish melody. Not because I am descended from the people of Málaga, but because I love the constant return to the same note, like a traveler returning home.

Or maybe it really is because I am Malagueña.

In 1907, my great-grandmother cradled her family and left her home in Málaga for dreams and for survival. Perhaps my DNA remembers this. Perhaps that's why I see her each morning when I reach the bridge. Perhaps the music conjures her up. Silly, I know. But still, I listen to Spanish guitar on my walk…just in case. A lone, brown leaf rides on the water, moving toward me from upstream, from a place where my ancestors laughed and cried. Individuals that I did not know yet are a part of me. They are the reason I'm able to stand here on this bridge. I make the sign of the cross, not because I'm particularly religious, but because this is the most reverent gesture I can think of. Do they see me? Can they feel my need to honor them?

I let gratitude swirl around me and stop with me on the bridge. And I think of them.

I hadn't known their story until the summer of 1998. That's when I met my Spanish cousins, and that's when I fell in love with Spain.

~ ~ ~ ~ ~

We touched down at Madrid's Barajas airport, and I was quite proud that my eleven years of Spanish enabled me to secure the rental car for my dad, my sister Jan, and me. We traveled south, through the congestion of Madrid then through the brown land of La Mancha on our way to the southern province of Andalucía. As we sped down the *autopista,* I grew more excited. Both sides of my family were from the south, and we'd soon be there. We practiced their complex names out loud.

The first destination was Málaga, home of my maternal grandmother. Thank goodness my dad kept the addresses of family he'd met when he and my mom went to Spain in 1969. Dad regretted that he hadn't kept in touch with them over the years. Different continents, different lives. Different branches of an old tree. Ever the methodical machinist, Dad tried to explain how each was related to us, but the branches of the tree were tangled, and even he couldn't quite explain it all. Finally, he summed it up simply, "All you need to know is that we're family. Cousins."

The long, green stretch of Parque de Málaga was a surprise after the parched land of La Mancha, but when we rolled down the windows and the scent of the ocean enveloped us, something tugged at me. I couldn't put my finger on it – a calm and yet an unease. I shrugged it off as we circled the same few blocks, then found a place to park.

We found the right high-rise apartment, and Dad knocked on the shiny wooden door. It swung open to reveal a woman in her seventies with curly silver hair and sparkling eyes. She wore a floral print dress with a white apron pinned at her shoulders. *How funny, that's just what my Grandma wore back home.* She dried her hands on a dishtowel and looked at us quizzically.

Dad explained who we were. Only one or two sentences had left his lips when Francesca broke into a huge smile and a sudden burst of staccato Spanish volleyed between the two of them. She pulled us into their "*piso,*" breathlessly telling two women inside of her great find. We were bombarded with hugs and kisses on each cheek.

While Dad talked with the women, Jan and I sat politely on a squishy couch covered in paisley. The small apartment smelled of fresh bread and ocean, as sheer curtains blew in from the veranda. We could see the sapphire Mediterranean just beyond the red tile roofs. Within thirty minutes the apartment swelled with nine more people, and the chatter was almost deafening. I turned to Jan, "Where did they all come from? Do you know what they're saying? I can only catch maybe fifty percent."

"You've got me beat," Jan said. "I can barely catch anything." We laughed as a young man came to our squishy couch, Spanish words spilling from his mouth like a waterfall. Without waiting for my rehearsed *"Por favor, hable mas despacio,"* beseeching him to slow his pace, he grabbed our hands and brought us to the dining room table. Chairs squeezed all around, and every inch of the table was covered with simple plates brimming with stewed peppers, chunks of bread, oily marcona almonds, thinly sliced *jamón*, *manchego* cheese, red chorizo, salted cod, and Dad's favorite, *"boquerones"* – marinated white anchovies. But my favorite was the plate of *"aceitunas."* I soon learned the marinated olives were ubiquitous throughout Spain, a constant you could depend upon at every table.

The cousins were curious. They smiled at me and Jan as they looked sideways to Dad and peppered him with questions. My father replied with sweeping hand gestures, animated expressions, and bursts of giggles. I had never seen him like this. He spun up, like a motor that had laid dormant and had finally been switched on. He was enchanted with the language and these people. And so was I.

Then we were off to Estepa, my grandfather's territory. Just an hour's drive north of Málaga, it seemed to be a world away. Just like I'd always seen in the pictures, this village was all tan earth and white walls, studded with bright flowers on balconies. Our family there was doing well. Brother and sister owned rival cookie factories and found themselves in good company. We learned this town is responsible for the famous cookies that proliferate Spain (and much of Europe) during the Christmas season. With more than thirty cookie factories, the faint smell of cinnamon and nuts blew through the town's streets.

We ate lunch at five patio tables strewn together along the sidewalk, while toddlers and teens and those hunched over their canes came to enjoy the celebration. My cousin, twenty years my senior, pulled me aside with a wink. We jumped into his truck and drove up to the iconic castle on the hill to enjoy the view of his many acres of olive orchards, his cookie factory and his restaurant that anchored a corner of the town. Pride rolled off of him as I marveled at his prosperity. But a shadow drifted across his eyes as he said, "Let's go see another place."

We tumbled along a dirt road and stopped at a well, shaded by trees, its stones crumbling where time had stolen its immortality. I had an uncanny feeling that I'd been there before, that I had looked across that land, all brown and green and splashed with sunflower fields. Perhaps I'd once had a dream of a similar place? My cousin told me of how his father and my grandfather would come to the well to share their dreams, boys looking to their future. But then my grandfather had gone with his parents on a journey to Hawaii in search of work and food and the chance of a better life.

My cousin said, "I'm so glad you've come. I'm so glad to know you." He fought back the tears, but mine slid down my cheeks and landed in small drops that stained the dirt beside the well.

Next, we ventured over Spain's Sierra Nevada mountain range, skirting Granada, and descending into a tiny white pueblo town. Aldeire made Estepa feel like the big city in comparison. Town was eerily quiet. Dad navigated us through a few narrow streets to a miniature plaza with a fountain where the trickle of water spilled from the mouths of four lions. Dad looked around like a dog on the scent, then he walked up one of the cobbled streets. Memory, instinct, or sixth sense – whatever it was, it worked. He knocked on a metal door, and when a woman answered, he began explaining in Spanish. "Carmen, I was here in 1969. I'm the nephew of Asuncion Montes, your cousin."

I thought the woman would faint as she put her hand on her heart. But then she cupped my father's face in her hands and cried. Carmen led us across the first floor where my dad recalled the pigs used to live. We ascended a spiraling staircase of ancient, black slate to a modern kitchen, complete with granite countertops, microwave oven, and drip coffee maker. We climbed another narrow staircase and emerged on a rooftop patio, half covered in thatch. Herbs hung drying on a rope beside a few fluttering towels. At the rustic table, we found her husband, Tomás, snapping green beans. "Tomás, look who I've found," she said, giddy with the excitement of family and the connection she had cherished so long ago.

My father's mother was fourteen when she left on a quest for a decent life. Her parents left everything and everyone they'd ever known, packed their meager belongings and their three children. But they left their fourth child behind. She was only five years old, my great aunt Asuncion, my "Tita Susie." Susie stayed with her cousin Carmen, and the two shared a childhood as sisters. But seven years later, once they settled in California, Susie's parents sent for her, and the two cousins were torn apart. I've often wondered where my Tita Susie considered her true home to be – her childhood against the mountains in Spain, or her adult life in the Bay Area of California.

Our final stop took us back to the outskirts of Málaga for a last goodbye. This time we sat around the table in my cousin's patio, heavy with the scent of jasmine. The table was covered in old photos and mementos, the olives, empty gazpacho bowls, and breadbasket pushed to the side. The photos told the story of the years my family had endured, first from the drought and poverty of the turn of the century, then of the oppression after the Nationalists were victorious in their bloody civil war. Scrawny children in ragged clothes. Drawn faces and sparse furniture. One of my oldest cousins in the room dabbed at her eyes with an embroidered handkerchief and said, "We had nothing. We were hungry. It was a very hard time."

I thought of my grandmother who left with her family when she was only six years old. I thought of the woman I knew - her gruff mood, her stout figure, and her round cheeks. I thought of her stucco house with the Spanish fans on the walls, and the figurines of bullfighters, and the castanets I played with as a child. I thought of her basement with its two bedrooms where so many family members had lived for a time, including my parents. I thought of that crystal candy dish on her coffee table that was always filled with sugared lemon drops. I thought of the spread of food we'd enjoy every Sunday, and I suddenly realized that marinated, Spanish olives were always there. The guilt gripped me. The shame for the good fortune I had enjoyed because my side of the family risked everything to board a ship and travel forty-seven days to an unknown land. For a chance. For a dream. For a desperate hope.

Cousin María Jesus must have seen my discomfort. She disappeared into the house, and a moment later emerged with two framed photos. She handed the first one to me. It was an image of her as a child in a beautiful white lace dress, her hands clasped reverently. "Your grandmother sent a communion dress for me. All the way from California. I'll never forget it."

"She did?" I replied, the words catching in my throat. I passed the photo to my sister.

"Your grandmother sent us boxes all the time," cousin Mari Loli chimed in. "Gosh, how we waited for those boxes." And the other cousins nodded and smiled. She went on, "She sent clothes. She sent little toys. She sent candy. We didn't know her, and we didn't understand where she was. But as kids, we knew we loved her. She was like our angel."

My sister and I wiped our tears with our napkins, and even my dad reached for his. Sniffles filled the patio as each of us felt the gravity of the moment.

Then she handed the second photo to me. The black and white image was very old, with a crease along the top. Three women stared back at me, two seated in chairs, and the third standing behind them. "This is our great-grandmother. Her name was María," Mari Loli pointed to the woman seated on the right. "And these are her sisters. Your great-grandmother, Bernarda, is this one," she said, pointing to the standing woman in her black dress and her hair pulled into a bun, barely visible at the back of her neck. It was only a photo, but I couldn't take my eyes off of hers. They seemed to talk to me.

I think my grandmother had always meant to go back to Spain, but by the time she was old enough, political tensions were on the rise. I think of the sadness she must have endured - the early childhood memories of her home, and how she had to leave it. How she sent packages back to her relatives she didn't know in a country she grieved for. Did she ever think of California as her home? I wish I'd had the wisdom to ask her when I could have.

As we drove back to Madrid, I knew I was forever changed by this trip to meet my Spanish family. Each stop held a similar experience, the loud and frenetic Spanish conversation, the sudden arrival of family spanning all ages, the table filled with simple, delicious tapas, and the stubborn negotiations as the Spaniards fought with each other to host the American cousins during our brief visit.

From table to table, olive to olive, it was the intimate conversations in the homes of our cousins that made me love this country and love these people – my country, my people. They'd drop everything, they'd leave work, and they'd cancel all plans to flock to the cousin's home who had won the battle to host us. They'd turn the pages of photo albums, pull mementos from boxes, and rattle off the stories of their lives. Farming, droughts, marriages, babies, wars, and heartbreaks. I asked questions, clarified my fragile understanding, and scribbled out multiple family trees. But how could I possibly capture with lines and letters the lives of these people? Their history became my history as the stories drifted by, generation to generation.

~ ~ ~ ~ ~

It's hard to believe that was almost twenty-three years ago.

Back home on my bridge, the Spanish guitar thrums in my ears. I look upstream, and I remember the stories I heard around the Spanish tables. I think of the challenges my ancestors faced in their time. And I realize I'm smiling. Are we so different? In my time, we have political drama, drought, floods, and disease. And immigrants still risk everything to create new lives.

My great-grandparents felt they had to leave their homes. My grandparents must have wanted to return home to Spain, but when they couldn't, they wanted their children to be American, to have them call the United States their home. And me? Of course, the US is my home, but I can't explain the sense I felt while in Spain. It was as if my soul knew it came from that land, that it belonged there. It too is home.

I wipe a cold tear away, and I watch the brown leaf in the water below, swirling in a dark eddy. I can't see Bernarda anymore, but she'll be there again tomorrow. She, and Spain, are part of me. Malagueña.

She Stayed: A Chronicle of Enduring Friendships

T-Ann Pierce

My friend was lamenting to her pharmacist. I stood off to the side, poking at lip balms and pocket-sized Kleenex packages, while my friend, shoulders slumped, conveyed her disbelief and frustration. The pharmacist had just informed her that her insurance company no longer covered the cost of her Hormone Replacement Therapy. I watched my friend deflate.

Begrudgingly, my friend handed over two hundred dollars for her Hormone Replacement Therapy, a smidge of estrogen and progesterone that, one month before, was a fraction of the price. HRT keeps her relatively normal. She'd rather chew her own leg off than parent two teenagers without it. It helps to even out her moods, which goes a long way in the arena of staying married and employed. It significantly reduces the amount of time she cries in the shower. HRT keeps her from sweating like a cold toilet on a hot day, and it resuscitates her lifeless libido; without it, the chances she wants to have sex hovers somewhere around zero. With it, her chances swell to a whopping six, maybe seven percent. Two hundred dollars is a small price to pay for those odds.

The two of us used to talk endlessly about exciting things. Back in the 80s, we associated excitement with one of two things: it either led to hangovers (say, for example, concerts, parties, and boys) or it carried a risk of pregnancy (say, for example, concerts, parties, and boys). We are now at an age where two glasses of wine consumed too quickly will leave us with debilitating hangovers. And birth control? Please. Our plumbing is coughing dust or has been removed altogether. Boys have been replaced by old men in airports who sidle up next to us and whisper suggestively, 'You are really rocking that gray hair.' They hit on us not because they want to do us but because they clock our sturdy frames and figure we're just the gal they need to hoist them onto the toilet after their next major medical event. Their behavior is insulting and hard to find flattering, but somehow I do.

When we first met, my friend and I had these gorgeous, plump, pinkish brains crammed with grooves and ridges designed to retain all the information needed to get into and out of college. Our young brains were like giant pieces of pasta that maximize sauce clingage. Back in the day, we actually memorized phone numbers. We remembered all the main characters in Judy Blume's book, Are You There God? It's Me, Margaret. We remembered to set split-flap alarm clocks every night. We remembered the name of that one guy in college who had the third nipple. We used to remember the names of our kids on the first try, but now our brains are saturated.

Today, our brains are not so plump and pinkish; they've shriveled with motherhood and menopause. Our brains are more grayish yellow than pink, like an ashtray full of Marlboro Lights butts. Once spongy and dense with folds, today, our brains are sodden with useless information. Decades' worth of song lyrics, commercial jingles, and Monty Python quotes have filled up and smoothed out our brains. Details float and bob aimlessly in our heads like a band of ten thousand little yellow rubber duckies lost on the ocean's rough swells. Motherhood and menopausal fog coated our brains like a slick layer of WD40, making it a comical scramble for any new information to stick; new bits of information, unprepared for slick conditions, splay out like a deer on ice. New information that actually sticks the landing is often spun into the cosmic abyss on its first or even second attempt at penetration. It is not unheard of for information to take three or more attempts before it is absorbed, retained, and recalled on demand. Except for a deal. We'll remember the price of any deal we ever got, no matter how long ago we got it.

Many conversations we share today are two-woman circuses. We jump through hoops of fire, trying to retrieve words. Because word retrieval is hard. So is remembering the point of a conversation. We are easily distracted now. It is hard to focus on the point of one conversation when we interrupt and blurt out reminders to talk about a completely different topic later. Sometimes, we must stop mid-conversation to shout disparaging remarks at the driver in front of us and comment on how all erratic driving today can be linked to the political candidate we do not support. Then, we lose track of where we were in the conversation. Occasionally, we get off topic because the server comes, and we stop talking and order green tea. Or someone has to go pee, so hold that thought. Or we simply forget the point of what we are talking about. And yet, we never run out of things to say.

A few years ago, this friend and I were on a girls' getaway in Maine, which turned out to be more Dumb and Dumber than Thelma and Louise. One night, I was driving the rental car through a rural, one-stop sign town going 40 mph in what I later found out was a 25. Blue lights flashed behind me. I pulled over. I suspect the young officer was prepared to find an impaired driver. Instead, he got two batty women with nothing but blueberry pie stuck between their teeth. He approached the car. We rolled down the windows and began talking at once about how sorry we were and how we weren't from there, and were bears and moose in the area because it was pretty dark and scary, how does anyone find where they are going in that kind of dark? And was the speed limit posted? Because I had no idea what the speed limit was and was he single? Because we knew just the girl for him. By the time we were done with him, he was exhausted. This is not how we got out of tickets when we were younger.

My friend and I have been friends long enough that we can, without a hint of embarrassment, announce, 'I'm going to shit myself if you don't pull this car over at the next gas station.' We burp. We pick wedgies. We share dressing rooms without self-consciousness. She doesn't judge my ill-fitting, pilled, and stretched-out bra. She doesn't notice the squishy, rippled remnants of the four children I've birthed. She doesn't care if I'm bikini-ready. Her face doesn't twist away in horror at the sight of the gnarly scar under my right arm where an unskilled doctor once yanked a tumor out of me like he was wrestling a sea cucumber from the ocean floor. My friend has my best interest in mind, so I trust her in the dressing room. She says things like: 'Terrible color,' 'Oh, God no,' or, 'That would be cute if you weren't old.' When something is flattering, she simply says, 'Buy it.' And I do.

Confident women stand where insecure teenagers used to be.

One of the most breathtaking aspects of age is the ushering in of confidence. Small positive actions, repeated over time, allowed us to trade in self-doubt for self-trust. We know ourselves now. We stopped trying to please so much. We know our strengths and accept most of our weaknesses; we're not trying to become world-class athletes or commercial artists. We aren't interested in sitting at the cool girls' table, though often we do. We are finally comfortable in our skin, thankfully. When we were younger, we were far too preoccupied with fitting in and trying to be everything to everyone. My friend recently revealed that before she had kids, she'd work 60-hour weeks. By the end of the week, she wanted nothing more than to collapse on the couch with her husband and order a Vietnamese takeaway. Instead, she felt obligated to join friends every Friday night. So, every Friday, she and her husband met up with four other couples for dinner. They'd meet at a predetermined restaurant and then go en masse to Blockbuster to choose a movie. Later, they'd return to one couple's house to watch the movie. Together. This group of ten. Every week.

My friend worried she'd have no friends if she said 'no,' if she took a break. She carried on being exhausted every Friday night to keep the peace. Today, if she were told she'd have to spend every Friday getting ten people to agree on a restaurant *and* a movie, she'd laugh so hard that tears would roll down her leg. She no longer sacrifices her soul for the sake of fitting in. She prioritizes herself and her family. She knows good friends aren't born simply of togetherness but of like-mindedness, loyalty, humor, acts of kindness, and space to breathe.

We have a group text with other high school friends. The five of us could not be more different. To look at us on paper, you'd never expect us to be friends, let alone confidants who connect daily. We share a lot of history, most of which occurred before the invention of smartphones (thank God). We 'get' each other, which is refreshing since our humor is, let's just say, not for everyone. This group text is free-flowing; there is no pressure and no judgment. We send memes and laugh-out-loud comments. No one keeps score. We exchange words of encouragement if one of us is facing a challenge. We rally if there has been a difficult diagnosis. We ache when someone's pet dies. We support each other as our kids grow and our parents' age. We reassure the first-time bride that she will be a gorgeous bride, menopausal midsection and all. We celebrate milestones. This 'little' text thread braces us from what life decides to throw at us.

I have cast a large net when it comes to friendships. I have grade school, high school, and college friends. I struck gold with previous neighbors. I have dear ones across the pond in England, where we lived for a time. I've got mom friends and women business owner friends. I've got book club friends, creative friends, and writing friends. I have friends I made while volunteering and at church. Heck, I've got virtual friends I've never even met in the flesh. I have never expected one person to complete me; the strain of that weight could make a person snap.

The common trait my friends share is their ability to be fairly self-sufficient. I'm not great with demanding, emotionally needy people. Pac-Man me, chase and chomp at my soul to feed your neediness or ego, and I'll check out like a fainting goat. My wildly varied collection of friends challenges me. They make me better. They call me out when I want to settle. They teach, they commiserate, they make me laugh, and they inspire me. On days that feel heavy and hopeless, and sadly, I've faced more than a few of those, my friends remind me that I take up space in this world and that I matter. When my husband suffered a stroke, and instantly, life became terrifyingly uncertain and bleak, my friends surrounded me with support. They filled my fridge. They carpooled. They lifted up prayers and sent good juju. Their hope vaccinated me against despondency and despair. I truly felt suspended in their grace. They tethered me to their sides, three-legged race style, and helped me toward a finish line none of us could see. This is what friends do. We hold, support, and shine a light in the dark so our dear ones can find their way.

Somedays, we are lucky enough to be the strong ones. Somedays, we need help or support. Friendships are not fully formed, not yet stitched together, until we've been on both sides of giving and receiving. Giving feels good. Receiving requires vulnerability. And vulnerability is terrifying. Vulnerability can feel torturous on its own, but often, vulnerability acts like a hurricane, spawning off tornadoes of other uncomfortable feelings, feelings like guilt, shame, or fear. Surviving a battering storm of raw emotions with a friend creates a bond. A friend who stands witness to your pain or grief or fear reflects back your belovedness. By showing up and being willing to sit with you in your discomfort, knowing they cannot remove your pain, knowing they cannot make you feel better, they declare your contribution to this world. You radiated friendship and unconditional love, which will now come back to you. You matter. Your life matters. You are worthy. To have a friend who is willing to be inconvenienced, share a burden, or hurt for us even when they cannot fix our pain or grief is a gift of a lifetime. It is a deeply humbling gift to rely heavily on friends from time to time. Accepting support from friends is like getting to experience our impact firsthand. Like George Bailey in It's A Wonderful Life, allowing our friends to deeply care for us emotionally, mentally, and physically gives us a rare glimpse into a well-lived life. I know a woman who was admitted to the hospital for an emergency surgery. She is an expert in her field. She is outgoing, easy to like, fun to be around, and brilliant. She has a huge network of mom-friends who stepped in immediately to help with her grade-school kids, but lying in that hospital bed sent her into a tailspin. She came to the painful realization that, despite enjoying a large circle of acquaintances, she didn't have friends she could call to sit by her bed and hold her hand quietly as she cried in fear. After she recovered, she made it her mission to reach out for more one-on-ones with her friends. She deliberately cultivated closer friendships, ones that went beyond convenience and fun, ones that created more connectedness and meaning in her life.

Society force-feeds us this notion that beauty is only for the young. The beauty industry hammers us with the message that we are not attractive if our skin is not taut and our lips are not pouty. Our knees should not droop, our décolletage should not crepe. I simply cannot understand these standards. It is bewildering. When I look at my friends, I see beauty through and through. Without hesitation, I can tell you my middle-aged friends are infinitely more beautiful today than they were in their youth. Age, experience, and wisdom suit them. I sometimes stare at my friends, completely distracted by their laugh lines. I love those lines, and further to that, I love that our shared experiences contributed to those lines on their faces; what a privilege. Women have humility, dimension, and depth that young girls don't. I don't know a soul who hasn't been through it by our age, and I find the newly exposed facets of wisdom, resilience, grace, and humor that show on my friends' faces undeniably attractive. There was a sameness we shared when we were young and wrinkle-free. We were hard to tell apart. We aged, and the victories, joys, pain, grief, and even summers in the sun etched onto our faces like a map of our lives. The beautiful smile of a young girl, innocent and unmarred by life, does not hit the same as that same girl, decades older, who has known both ecstasy and excruciating pain. Give me the smile of a woman who has fiercely protected herself and the ones she loves, who climbed literal and/or proverbial mountains, and who still chooses to laugh. Give me the smile of a woman who has the wisdom of lived experiences, who has an aggregate of perspectives, and who is willing to sit in the tension between them. *That* smile is disarmingly beautiful.

Admittedly, maintaining friendships is not always for the faint of heart. Lack of friendships, disconnection, and strained friendships can feel all-consuming. Social media pressures us to have 'perfect' lives, making us believe that our relationships and friendships should always be easy. We can fall into comparison traps. We can start keeping scores of who initiates conversation more, who is busier, who tries harder, and who can better prove her commitment to the relationship. We can let the inequity of bank accounts divide us. We can take things too personally. Or we look on socials and believe everyone else has a posse of ride-and-die besties, and we, with our hodge-podge crew of loose friendships, aren't doing friendship 'right.' Maybe our busy lives or maybe the pain we suffered in previous friendships keep us from nurturing friendships today. Cultivating friendships can seem futile, too vulnerable, and downright exhausting. But we don't need friends that live in our back pockets. We don't need friends we see every day or even every week. With loneliness at epidemic rates, we simply need a couple of people who make us feel seen, heard, and valued. We need friends who lift our souls: think easy. Think undemanding. Think light. We need one or two friends we can connect with honestly and wholeheartedly without squeezing too hard. It was the band 38 Special who said it so eloquently, 'Just hold on loosely, but don't let it go.'

Ancient Sicilians had a word to describe a lifelong female friendship that has grown and deepened with time: 'cummari.' Cummari was used as an alternative to the word 'godmother;' it also described a bride's maid of honor. It comes up in word and song to describe the bond between women whose relationship feels like family. It is meant for a woman who, by some unknown grace, walked into our life and never left. Despite our flaws, our misgivings, and our brokenness, she stayed. To be a cummari is to be chosen and trusted for a lifetime. If the word cummari isn't enough to fill your heart and water your eyes, just wait. There's more. Ancient Sicilians gifted female friends a basil plant when that friend crossed the threshold, becoming her cummari. How blessed would we be to reach the end of our rich and varied life, knowing there was at least one woman who stood witness to the best and worst of our lives? I can't even…Someone, please hand me a tissue.

Friendships don't endure easily or without intention. Priorities might shift. Incomes may not be equal. Our friendships might not always look pretty or feel easy. We might clash occasionally. Our parenting styles might not mesh. We might not always be in the same stage or place. We may differ, but day by day, we can choose each other. We can choose to link arms with our cummari through thick and thin. I suspect that at some point in our journey, we'll pause and mentally replay the story of our lives. It is then we might notice for the first time how every time we were together, our friend helped us heal from the wounds other people carved in our souls. We might wince, recalling heartbreaks. We might laugh out loud. Our hearts might swell with gratitude. We'll undoubtedly feel the jarring, wind-buffeting effect of time whooshing past at high speeds. It may occur to us that it turns out that this whole time, we weren't just relishing each other's humor or relying on her wisdom. We weren't just connecting or commiserating. Together, we were covering a whole lot of ground. We were, in fact, walking each other home.

The Paradox of Progress: Finding Joy in Going Back

Amber Field

Sometimes, in order to move forward, you have to go backwards.

In 2016, I was working for a tech start-up in Washington, DC. The company had a great mission: we used behavioral science (i.e., good peer pressure) to encourage energy conservation by sending reports comparing households' energy usage with their neighbors'. It was an effective way to inspire neighbors to "keep up with the Joneses"–but for a good cause. Turning off your air conditioner and using a fan to cool your home may seem like a step back in technological progress, but if an entire neighborhood does it, we collectively drive positive change and move towards a cleaner future together. One step backwards on the technology track equals two steps forward on the climate track.

I'd just earned a promotion at the company to my first management role, leading our Program Management Office. This was a significant career leap forward for me, and I was proud of the new position. Plus, the work environment was exhilarating! Everyone knows about the famous amenities at large tech companies like Google and Facebook: slides between floors, free food, video games, and nap pods. Our office was like that but on steroids. We had free chair massages on Wednesdays, snacks galore, celebrity speakers, and even an engineering offsite for three days in Las Vegas. When we were at work, we were all focused, having fun, and making a difference. It was intense, but very fulfilling.

Balancing work with my personal life, however, was daunting. With two young daughters and a husband at home, my days began at 5 a.m. with a run, followed by getting the kids ready for daycare, an hour-long commute, a full workday, and another long commute home. Evenings were all about the kids. My husband worked too, and we barely saw each other. Weekends were consumed by chores, and our vacation time was spent visiting family in the Midwest.

The new management role immediately proved to be more challenging than I'd imagined. In the first six months, I dealt with a colleague who complained about my promotion over him all the way up the chain to our CEO, lay-offs, restructuring, and then the worst thing possible happened.

The company announced that it was being bought by Oracle, a large, bureaucratic behemoth of an organization with a reputation for dismantling its acquisitions. I decided to leave.

My position at that start-up had been such a point of pride in my life, and without it, I felt a bit lost. It was a feeling that had been growing sneakily in all aspects of my life, hidden at the back of my mind until a major life change forced it to the surface. I wondered when I had last felt like myself.

I grew up in a small suburb of Milwaukee, WI. The population of the entire town was 12,000, and my graduating class had only 99 students, most of whom stayed in the Milwaukee area, married their high school sweethearts, and had a few kids.

After high school, I moved to the state capital for college at the University of Wisconsin-Madison. I *loved* Madison. The city is nestled between two beautiful lakes, with the state capitol, downtown, and college campus squeezed onto an isthmus, providing endless opportunities for learning, entertainment, and outdoor pursuits. I did academically well there, had friends, activities I cared about, and a great life. I would have stayed in Madison forever, but I got a job at IBM in Minnesota after college. I married my high school boyfriend, and we moved around for five years while I worked remotely, eventually landing in a suburb of Washington, DC. Getting a college degree, my first job, and living in an exciting new city all seemed like forward progress to me. I was right on track for the stereotypical American Dream: work hard for 40 years, get married, buy a home, have kids, and live happily ever after.

Life in DC offered world-class museums and a vibrant cultural scene, but you had to fight traffic to do everything. The constant grind of full-time work and long commutes left little time for personal pursuits. At some point during my six years there, I started to dream of a simpler, more fulfilling life. I wanted to sell most of our material possessions, buy a smaller house, and reduce my hours at work. I dreamed of becoming an author but had no time to write. I also wanted to live internationally with my family so that my kids could learn a foreign language, but we were so entrenched with our daily lives that this seemed like an impossible goal. I'd always wanted to have a bit of an unconventional life, and instead, I was living an overly conventional one. There was no time for my dreams, only time to uphold the frantic life I'd built around me. I wasn't sure how to make forward progress anymore, but I had one idea.

When I suggested moving back to Wisconsin for a better quality of life, my husband said no. We spent years discussing it, but in the end, I lost that argument. My needs were not as important as his career goals.

So, I moved to Madison anyway, leaving my now ex-husband behind in DC.

The move seemed like a big step backwards. Why would I want to move from the exciting East Coast to the Midwest where I was born? I accepted a pay cut, downsized from a four-bedroom home to a two-bedroom apartment, became a single mom, and shifted from senior management back to project management. I got a divorce and lost half of my net worth. All of these were huge steps backwards.

Except…they brought me immense personal satisfaction. In one fell swoop, I got rid of my commute, extraneous material possessions, house maintenance, and an unhealthy relationship. Maybe my career and home life would suffer forever, but maybe I could be satisfied with a new kind of life, a quieter one back home in Wisconsin.

That was seven years ago and a lot can happen in seven years.

My career in Madison began flourishing unexpectedly. I loved my new company, and it loved me. Within a couple of years, I was promoted to a Director role, then Vice President, overseeing all of our product and engineering teams, which was roughly half the company. My salary tripled. I rarely needed to work overtime, and I had plenty of flexibility to care for the girls. My commute was twelve minutes door-to-door if I walked.

I reconnected with old friends and organizations. At a UW-Madison Computer Science alumni event, I met the new chair of the Computer Science Department. We started talking, and a year later, I had developed and was teaching a new course, the Computer Science Capstone. Last year, I published a book for the course. Four years ago, I met an amazing man, the most supportive guy I know, and married him two years later.

That brings me to today. Two months ago, I quit my full-time job as Vice President without having another one lined up. Despite the financial setbacks associated with my divorce and the move home, I achieved financial independence. Life is simply a lot less expensive in the Midwest. One major lesson my time in the DC area taught me is that time itself is far more important than things or money, especially when you've got enough of both. I wanted more time to volunteer, teach, write, spend with my kids, and travel. I'm writing this story from an apartment in Florence. A week after I quit, we left town and traveled to London, Bath, Manchester, Edinburgh, Rome, Cinque Terre, and Florence.

Reflecting on the last decade, I realize that I wouldn't be where I am today without dismantling the life I once knew–a life that by any external measure seemed nearly perfect. What appeared to be a huge step backward at the time was actually a giant leap forward toward a life I love. I owe it all to having the courage to take that step and move back home.

Welcome Home

Laurie Riedman

As a child, I didn't know that my home differed from anyone else's. It was my home. It was exciting to live where we lived. I had no idea it was dangerous. It was just fun to live in a junkyard.

There was so much to explore around me, untethered and free. I grew up in rural Connecticut in the 1960s and 1970s, when mothers shooed their children outside as soon as possible—especially during the summer months—having no care or idea where they were all day.

Ahhhhhh, the delicious freedom of getting lost for so many hours. We'd emerge as if we were drunk and dazed by the power of pretend. Just as the sun sank in the sky, we'd drag ourselves home, hungry and happy.

We found our share of mischief, that is for sure, as there was no shortage of it where I lived.

Our home was a simple cedar-shingled square smack dab in the middle of my dad's junkyard. It was one of the only solid things in my life at the time. Dad built it in stages utilizing second-hand windows secured from homes that were being torn down, left-over lumber, and other odds and ends.

Instead of a white picket fence, shrubbery, and a lawn, twin peaks of used tires surrounded our house, black rubber mountains towering over us, and several piles of mismatched hubcaps waiting for some poor soul to pick through to find the mate to the one lost on some roadway. A babbling brook wove behind the house and all along one side of the junkyard as if it didn't quite belong there.

To use kids living in a junkyard was pure heaven. What was there not to love?

Somedays, we were explorers on a treasure hunt. We'd escape deep into the junkyard, prying open trunks and rusted car doors to flip dirty floor mats and peek in glove compartments to see what amazing things we might find. We found treasures of some sort in everyone!

On other days, we were artists, stepping back from the many junk piles to secure just the right item and shape we needed to create a sculpture. Remembering them now, I'm pretty sure they could be mistaken today for a modern metal cairn. Instead of perfectly round and balanced rocks making a zen-like cairn, we created metal ones with oddly shaped metal car parts (sometimes trucks and even old bus parts) piled up and precariously balanced. We cleverly used rusted-out wheel rims (they were pretty heavy and made an excellent base). We'd pull out wires and springs that we had no idea what part of the car they went to, using them to tie other bits on top of one another. Oh, the finishing touch of our masterpieces was often a decorative and shiny hubcap.

Other times, we became race car mechanics. We tried hard to build a go-cart seriously, but the bits and pieces we tried to use wouldn't stay together. Perhaps it was because, at the age of 8, we couldn't get the gas blowpipe on Dad's welder to light. *Thank goodness!*

As I made friends in school and accepted a few invites to friends' homes, I realized how unique our living situation was. Our Dad didn't come "home from work" and set his briefcase on the oriental carpet, taking his "work shoes" off by the door as he lovingly announced, "Honey, I'm home." No, my dad's uniform was navy blue work pants with a matching button-down shirt with his name "Bob" embroidered on the pocket. He was likelier to sit his ass down at the dinner table and yell, "I'm hungry. What the hell is for dinner"?

The home my friend's dad walked into after work was tidy and put together. It looked more like the rooms in the ladies' magazines I studied at the beauty parlor while waiting for my grandma to have her weekly cut and set appointment.

Our home was clean but could have been a bit tidier. I loved it just as it was. Let's just say it had more of an early Salvation Army / Italian vibe. (Our living room featured a plastic-covered floral couch with a fluted tufted back—a hand-me-down from my mom's Italian/Spanish parents.) The room's showstopper was a large Magnavox console TV with stereophonic speakers on each side: Mom and Dad's pride and joy. Enough said; you get the picture.

I don't remember when, but at some point, I quit inviting some friends to my house. It was because of something I had figured out: *the one-time rule.* I decided that there must be some rule my Mom and I weren't familiar with that meant friends could only visit my house once.

You see, what usually happened was this:

As a mom (or dad) drove down their child for a playdate at our house, they first encountered our steep dirt driveway. While driving - nose down the driveway, the dirt kicked up by the shiny wheels of their new model cars swirled around them, forming a dust cloud. As they stopped at the base of the driveway, the dust settled slowly, revealing our home smack dab in the middle of a junkyard. I imagine the image slowly being revealed just as whatever is behind curtain number 1 is revealed by Vana White on the Price is Right or how the scene in a snow globe suddenly comes into view after a vigorous shake.

After talking to my mom, the parents eventually allowed their child to stay for the pre-determined play date. Walking back to their car with quizzical looks as if they were wondering if their child would survive until pick-up time, they'd turn their cars quickly around, tires spinning, and sped up the hill, leaving, yes, another dust cloud in their wake.

More often, this would be the only time their child could play at my house. There were exceptions, as I had my share of good friends who came over more than once. Those kids were my tribe. Yet, this *one-time rule* helped soften the situation that occurred with *the other kids*. It was hard for me, as a child, to understand what was wrong with where I lived. To wonder what was wrong with me. To me, the junkyard was a magical place. Who wouldn't want to hang out with me there?

Years later, as I entered those tumultuous pre-teen years when hormones fueled my every social move as if it were a chess game and created the pressure and desire to "fit in" at any cost, it was then my childhood blinders were removed, and shame took its place.

From then on, I was ashamed of where I lived and only invited a few. I'd find ways to meet friends in other places in town. Or get rides to their homes. I found ways to pretend I didn't live where I lived. The magic of the junkyard wore out and became tarnished as I aged.

Fast-forward several decades. I am married and lovingly restoring an Italianate Victorian home in the Finger Lakes of New York with my husband, Rich. We are raising three daughters and building several successful businesses.

We spent most of our extra cash and time painstakingly repairing it room by room. We re-tiled floors, replaced wallpaper with much more pleasing "period appropriate" designs, put up tin ceilings, repaired old slat and plaster walls, discovered cool pocket doors hidden inside a wall, stripped our massive front door that had to be at least 3 inches thick, and so much more. Over several decades, we spent every weekend creating a beautiful home filled with period antiques and just the right modern amenities.

My home became a place I was proud of. A home where we welcomed friends and family without hesitation. A home that our children could invite their friends to. Even as I write this, a calm sense of satisfaction washes over me as I recall how we did it. We created a home that became the "hang-out" place when our kids became teens. Our home was the location for filming creative videos, rehearsing science presentations, and "studying" for school exams. Or - just hanging out on a lazy, hot summer afternoon.

I worked at home in an office upstairs, and I'd often come downstairs to find our living room filled with a group of kids. When I walked past, I'd see our children's friends lounging, feet hanging over the edge of the couch or sprawled out on the carpet as if it were their own home. It touched something that made me smile on the inside to see this. They felt welcome in our home. Our home was their home. That was what I desperately needed and wanted our home to be.

Our home healed me. Or rather, by creating our home, I healed myself.

I admit that there was a period when I was bordering on compulsive about creating just the right home. This was what I refer to as my "materialistic" phase. I was even obsessed. I often joked my inner "Martha Stewart" was taking control. Yet, it wasn't always about how our home looked but how it felt to me and those who entered it. I desperately needed it to be welcoming. For others to feel "at home" and at ease there. Creating our home - of being obsessed with perfecting it - was an act of healing.

With each remodeling project, each antique purchased and purposely placed; our home became closer to the homes I remembered being in when visiting friends or those I had seen with awe so beautiful in those magazine pictures. But that didn't create the "feeling at home" energy I wanted. I think it was because I eventually felt like I belonged there as the years went on. I felt more comfortable. Thus, those who entered our home felt that comfort, too.

At each dinner party, kids gathering, and holiday open house we hosted, a little bit of that childhood shame flaked off. Each time someone came into our home and told me what a lovely and inviting home I had, another piece of childhood shame was released- transformed. Eventually, I didn't need that big home anymore. The stuff surrounding me that I lovingly collected and arranged became too much.

After 34 years of living there, raising three amazing daughters to become strong women, building two successful businesses, and healing my childhood traumas with a man I am more in love with today than when we walked down the aisle almost 37 years ago, I was able to say goodbye to that house.

My husband and I moved into a smaller, new townhome two years ago. Interestingly enough, we are simplifying our lives and, subsequently, our home. Slowly and purposefully, we curate just the right things that feel and fit us and the space. Our house is spacious, just like this phase of our lives. Once again, our home reflects who we are and what we need.

Home is healing. All my homes throughout my life have helped me come home to myself. The junkyard instilled in me the power of pretend and how it became a resilience that, quite frankly, saved me. Our lovingly restored Victorian helped me heal the childhood shame I picked up in the Junkyard – allowing me to recycle that shame into a source of love, connection, and joy. Restoring that home rehabilitated me, room by room. Working to create a welcoming and beautiful home as an adult, wife, and mother healed me.

And now, as I sit writing overlooking the lake from the deck of our new townhome, I resonate with the peaceful, calm, and simple life we are working to develop as we retire.

These realizations give new meaning to the mat outside my door. It says: "Welcome Home".

He Chews His Water

Susan Walter

Is this what my friends are talking about? New schedules and old habits mixed with revelations and old comforts?

I sat across from Bill for a late lunch in quiet comradery. Idling, he had finished his meal but remained engrossed in some breaking news article on his newsfeed.

He chewed on a sip of water.

This chewing, on water, is a habit at least as old as our 35 years together. Often noted but now noticed, it includes other non-chewable items, in my opinion.

We bumped into each other often during the two years of work-from-home mandates. Instead of commuting we rode bikes. Instead of mid-morning text exchanges we met in the corner of the kitchen for coffee (him) or tea (me). Instead of taking lunch alone, we asked, "Do you want me to make you something, too?"

Morning was later. Afternoon was vague. The dog got a lot of walks, too.

One day Bill felt logy after a longer weekend bike ride. He excused himself for a lie-down. Hours later, feeling worse, he reported stiffness, headache, muscle soreness, and high fever. The covid test was negative. Perhaps the flu? That was odd, I thought, because we haven't been near anyone. I called his doctor's office. However, no one wanted to see him out of an abundance of caution. "Treat him at home. Repeat the covid test tomorrow. Fluids and rest."

By morning his major joints had swelled beyond his ability to get out of bed. The maneuvering took almost 45 minutes. He has rheumatoid arthritis, mostly controlled by medications, and it wasn't too surprising that his joints swelled with illness. But the extent and pain level were beyond excruciating. This was concerning.

By the next day an unsatisfactory phone call with his rheumatologist, who yet insisted it was probably covid, was now insufficient. "Take him to the ER if you think it's that bad," he said to get me off the phone.

So I did.

~

I had been reluctant. He had to be bad enough for me to willingly take him to the only local hospital we dubbed the Hillbilly Heights Hospital. A place of last resort in our smallish town.

"Not covid," they confirmed in the emergency department. "Not the flu, either." Checking off easy suspects, they also cultured his blood.

Sepsis. Bacteremia. Streptococcus pyogenes. "Though we don't know how the infection started, we think it might have affected his ICD, the pacemaker/defibrillator implanted and wired into a chamber of his heart. We suggest surgery to remove it."

"Oh no, they're not," I thought, "No one at the Hillbilly Heights Hospital is doing cardiac surgery on him."

I paid upfront for an exorbitant, 2-hour, midnight ambulance ride to deliver him to his real cardiologists at the university hospital where he could receive better, if not the best, care considering the circumstances.

By the next day we gathered around a screen. "Wow," they said pointing to the screen. "Look at the images. He has *bio-vegetation*."

Curious, I peered at the images. A blobby tether ball wiggled and swung to and fro inside his heart's ventricle as his blood flowed through one chamber of his heart to the next. Pump swish, wiggle-wiggle. Pump swish, wiggle-wiggle. It vibrated with the beats. The infection blob, this *bio-vegetation*, was perhaps a generous half inch in diameter. Like a tether ball, it clung from one of the ICD lead wires that had been implanted in his heart years ago. The lead wire was a part of him, scar tissue keeping it embedded in his heart.

My heart, I thought. The one I've occupied since we were in college. The one that puts up with me, loves me, wakes with me each morning.

The defibrillator implant has done its job, too. It has shocked him back alive twice already, saving him from certain death. And now they tell me it needs to come out. The very thing that saves him can't do its job any longer. But first, the surgeon raised one finger, the bio-gunk needed to be carefully cleaned out. That blobby sack of streptococcus had infected the heart when it accumulated on the wire, infiltrated his blood, and made his body deathly ill. The *bio-vegetation* blob was the root cause of his illness, and dangerous.

"We have an alternative defibrillator implant to replace the old one. The lead wires won't be threaded *into* his heart like the one we are removing. Instead, the lead wires on this new one will stay outside his ribs, just under the skin. It's a 'Sub-Q' or subcutaneous. Less chance of re-infection," they assured me.

Meanwhile, my husband, never an ideal, compliant patient in the best of times, spent weeks in delirium, hallucinations, and cranky moods. One day he solved math problems on an imaginary blackboard. Another he strummed an invisible guitar, his fingers finding chords for music only he could hear. Food didn't appeal. Day was night. Night was day. He didn't care. Time reported only to the hospital's shift changes. It was many days before he could bend his elbows again, sit in a chair, or summon enough energy for someone to help him shower.

~

Here we are again, I mused. Back home sitting across the kitchen table from each other in our default seats. I regarded Bill. 60 pounds lighter. Not quite finishing a light lunch. A sweater despite the warm day. Later we'll walk around the block. Maybe venture twice around if he's up to it. A nap in between.

I looked at the clock. It's time. I prepared the syringe, alcohol wipes, and sterile gloves.

"Time for my medicine already?" Bill noted the medical paraphernalia.

"Yes, it's been 8 hours." I moved to sit near him. "Are you finished with your lunch?"

"Almost," he pushed his plate away, sat upright, and presented his central line for the intravenous antibiotics.

On the mend. My partner in problem solving and adventure. He lifted his glass for one last gulp.

He chews his water.

Cutting Flowers in My Mother's Garden

Katherine Cartwright

Among Her Things

It was a week ago that we had my mother's funeral.

I'd come to Washington because she was in the hospital, and by the end of the week she had died. This was not what I expected when I got here. Sometimes death comes quickly and unexpectedly, and I think it might always be a shock.

I've spent the last few weeks at my mother's house. I feel close to her here, among her things. Where I sometimes catch a breath of her scent. Where I turn around and see in my mind's eye a scene from a memory. Where I can pick up something and feel her. Where I prepare a meal in her kitchen and feel her with me, laughing.

I'm taking a few things home with me. I wonder how they will fit into my house, into my life. I'm not quite ready to let go of the house that was home to five generations of my family. That held our celebrations. That I've known as home since my birth when it was my grandparents' house.

There is so much to think about, to reflect on, to get used to. When I think about writing about it, I feel overwhelmed. So, I decided just to start writing. One piece of writing will never hold everything, just a piece of the story. The empty page feels like a canvas. My words, brush strokes. An image begins to emerge from the space and the color.

I'm not yet sure what I see.

Drying My Wings

The list is long.

I'm getting ready to leave my mother's house and head home after these threshold weeks. It feels like a new world that needs new maps. I'm not sure what to expect. What to find. How I will be with all of it. These weeks have been a chrysalis and I have come completely undone. I know the next step is to break the seam and emerge. Dry my wings. Fly.

From flower to flower. Gathering nectar and pollen to nourish and create.

It's the right season for it.

Moisture hangs heavy on the green in my mother's garden. Flowers that were coming into blossom when I arrived are spent. Peony. Azalea. Rhododendron. Mountain laurel. Even the first blooming of roses is spent. But there will be more. The spiderwort continues to bloom. When I come next week there may be hydrangeas. I would like to see one more blossoming of Mom's hydrangeas.

There are many lists. Not just the one that lets me know I've done everything I need to do before I get in the car and drive away.

Mom always stood at the back door, waving and calling, "I love you!" as we drove away.

And if I am truthful, I will admit that each time I left in these last years, I took a long look just in case it would be the last time I would see her standing there. And the last time was the last time. That was April 29. Another Friday.

I drove away, waving to my mother as she stood on the threshold of her house. Three weeks later I held her hand as she stood on the threshold of life and death. Today I'll cross the threshold of the house again for the drive back home and it will be empty for the first time when I look back. I'll cross the threshold at home, and everything will be different there too. These days of threshold crossings leave me so much to reflect on. I've felt cocooned here, cushioned a bit from it all.

I notice that when I use phrases like "it all," I've hit my edge and it's time to lay down the work for the day. Tomorrow I'll be writing from a different place, with a different view, at a different table. My most familiar writing spot.

But I wonder as I sit here today in the place I always considered a change-of-scenery during my writing projects, whether that will be a world-turned-upside-down too.

Tree of Life

Everything feels weird.

Home does not feel like home. The few little things I brought home from Mom's seem strange and disconnected in my space. Of course, truthfully, things are a mess. I lit out of here very quickly almost three weeks ago, leaving a bit of chaos behind me. There are boxes and bags of recycling that need to go out. My kitchen table is covered with paper and dishtowels and books, and mail I need to go through. I haven't unpacked from my trip yet. I did water the plants. They were hanging on for dear life.

I feel strange. Not quite right in my body. This morning, I lost it. Lots of tears. I felt inconsolable and deeply alone.

I went to my dresser, to a box Mom gave me in 2015. It was filled with things she made for me that had messages attached – mother/daughter connection-type messages. The box once held a gift that my daughter gave her grandmother several years before Mom repurposed it to hold a gift for me.

It makes a beautiful kind of circle.

And I think she made it for just this time.

One Small Thing

Yesterday it was flowers, and a trip to the store to buy ingredients for a nice meal I'll share with my son today.

With grief, the landscape changes moment to moment. Distraction does not work for me. I need space to feel my feelings, to map the changing topography. What does work is creating space for life-giving things, even small ones, like three beautiful stems of lily or three vibrant sunflowers or taking apart a sweet onion with a nearly perfect dice and concentration on my knife work.

Releasing the fragrance of fresh dill or a juicy lemon. Seeing the beauty of a savory pilaf come together and then adding just a bit of dried apricot to tease out some sweetness.

To tease out some sweetness.

I'm thinking about the sweet things in life today, and about balance. I'll work some today and play some. Spend some time with my son, making and savoring a beautiful meal and a nice glass of wine. It's a chardonnay. I didn't think I liked them, but while I was away a few months ago, researching California Central Coast organic and biodynamic wines, I discovered this bottled sunshine.

I hope it tastes as good at home as it did under the pergola at the vineyard.

Unpacking a Photograph

There was a long shelf in my mother's living room where she kept the wedding pictures of her children.

Mine was still there, even though I've been divorced for almost ten years. It's a photograph that echoes one of my grandmother as a bride, long white gown with the train sweeping around me. My attendants' bouquets encircle me. I think it was probably a popular pose in the 80s, one I wanted to make sure the photographer took. I was young and hopeful for all the beauty and wonder of life and love and of building a life and family together.

Mom kept that memory for me.

When my husband and I separated, I put the wedding album and all the framed photographs we had in our home away in a large bin. The bin is in storage along with bins that have many of our other family photographs. It was too difficult in those days to look at them. To see what had died.

But I love that my mother kept the memory of the girl who stood on the threshold of all the wonderful things in life, who was radiant with joy and ready to step into a new expression of her life. In my mother's house it was one of many beautiful family memories.

I can't help but think I am standing on another threshold as I grieve the death of my mother.

Bereavement is liminal space. An old life has ended. The landscape of the new is not clear. There is a radical reorientation of everything. New maps are being drawn. Literally.

There is something this writing wants to capture today – the way a photograph captures a moment in time and makes it live forever.

Love is risky. We know that the people in our lives come and go. To love them is to acknowledge that one day we will lose them. But we still take the risk. We open ourselves to loving and to being loved.

Yesterday I unpacked the photograph and set it down quickly. Charlie was coming for lunch and there was food to prepare and the table to set and time to spend together. This morning, I walked into the living room and picked up the framed photo and held it in my hand.

It was a living thing in my mother's house, a piece of a larger family story. I'm not sure what it is today, or where it belongs.

Mending the Heart

Everyone has been so kind.

There have been invitations – dinner last night and tonight, lunch tomorrow. All prepared by friends at home. Someone stopped by the office yesterday with roses, freshly cut from her garden and fragrant. She also brought a small gift bag with tiny bottles of essential oils and a small packet of tea. Chamomile Comfort.

When I came home from work yesterday, my arms overflowing with gifts and kindness, I saw a box on the step and the corner of a greeting card envelope in the mailbox. The box was from my favorite chocolatier – Kakawa Chocolate House in Santa Fe. Friends in one of my writing groups remembered. The card was from someone whose mother died a few years ago. She remembered the love and support given to her during that time and offered it to me. It's a beautiful circle, that kind of connection.

When I came home from Mom's almost a week ago, my footfalls on the hardwood floors echoed like sounds in an ancient abbey. I move through my space as if it has somehow become strange and a little unrecognizable. There has been a shift at home that mirrors the shift in my larger sense of home.

My brothers and I have been talking a lot lately. I think we are weaving connections to bind up the places that have been rent. That word. I always think of something Jeremiah said in the Bible, "Rend your hearts and not your clothing." Isn't that what grief does? Rend the heart?

I was talking on the phone last night to a friend whose husband died suddenly last weekend. He asked what I was doing to take care of myself. I told him that mostly I am trying to be attentive to my heart. That there actually is something called "broken heart syndrome." Takotsubo cardiomyopathy can follow an extreme stressor, like the death of a loved one, especially in women over 50. It turns out that you can die of a broken heart.

The people who love me are getting it right. Fragrant, freshly cut roses from the garden, beautifully crafted dark chocolate truffles, lovingly prepared meals and company, a flood of cards, essential oils and teas, phone conversations and so many other things that remind me that I am not alone.

You see, for most of us, our mothers are the first and most constant source of love in our lives. Even before we draw our first breath, we live under her heart and her heartbeat is our first language.

When that disappears from the world, what then?

Death Is Not Done with Me Yet

The day is a bridge between places again, between rivers of my life, between . . . just between. Tonight, after a full day during which I must somehow squeeze in some packing and tidying and watering my plants, I'll drive back to Washington, back to Mom's house, and into the space of death and family grief once again.

My aunt died two years ago, a casualty of COVID-19, when she was unable to get a surgery she needed because medical resourcing was dedicated almost exclusively to meeting the challenges of the pandemic. My aunt and uncle had been planning their

50th anniversary celebration. Her death, just weeks shy of their anniversary, was a cruel irony.

I remember writing a tribute the morning after she died. I wrote about the open space of grieving that the pandemic demanded, as families were unable to come together to support each other, to celebrate, and to bury loved ones. I wrote about the sheer bewilderment of my uncle as he was left with the solitary task of planning a celebration of my aunt's life (someday) instead of the partnered planning of a celebration of their life together.

Then we all waited.

Waited for the pandemic to end. (It hasn't.) For the right time to gather to celebrate my aunt's life and to grieve together. (Is there an obvious "right time"?) For the confusion of the new landscape to begin to clear and show us its markers as we find our way through unfamiliar territory.

More than a month ago, my uncle decided it was time. We set the date. June 12. We began to make plans. A beautiful memorial celebration at their home with family and close friends. There would be food and flowers and storytelling, and the wearing of bright colors instead of the dark shades of bereavement. I began to think about what a memorial two years after a death might look like. How to celebrate, remember, honor, and grieve now, without taking us all back into the days just after her death and into the immediacy of it all. I began to pull together readings and prayers and poetry.

What was it? A week or two later that my mother went into the hospital, and then died a week after that, and then a week later the funeral and burial, and a week later the trip back home (for me), and now another week later and I am going back and our family, still raw with my mother's death, will gather again to remember and celebrate my aunt?

I pause. Close my eyes. And breathe.

And we will . . . show up again for each other and for what life and love call us to.

Skirting the Rabbit Hole of Things

I am back in my mother's house.

This morning, while writing, I am distracted by the many things that remain here, even with her gone.

And it is not simply the things I can touch.

But also, the things that touch me.

I pause the writing and begin to move around the room. And then I return.

There are times, in the morning writing, that I drift away or fall away or slip down some kind of rabbit hole of thought.

Today it is something else, as I rise and pick up this thing, or draw my fingers across that thing, or pause and touch a memory attached to something else.

But in returning to the page, I skirt the rabbit hole of things and return to myself.

Little Pleasures

I had lunch with a friend last week.

She made a yummy poached fish with herbs. She also offered some really nice water – one steeped with cucumber and mint and the other with lemon.

I ordered some pretty carafes today to make flavored water. There are three in the set. One for cucumber and mint, which I'd never thought to put together, one for lemon and basil, and another for some kind of fruit and herbs, probably berries or peaches or whatever else might be in season as the summer goes on. I like strawberry and basil together. I'm thinking of trying tarragon with something.

We planted herbs around the house this year. My landlady died on Epiphany and her son bought the house and moved into the apartment downstairs. I asked if he'd mind if I planted herbs out front. He thought it was a great idea and said he'd see about planting tomatoes in the backyard in pots or a raised bed.

The spring was unseasonably cold and wet and by the time there was sun enough and warm temperatures to plant the herbs, I had left for Washington to be with Mom in the hospital. I thought I'd be there a few days and it turned out to be almost three weeks.

When I came back, Bob had planted the herbs and flowers, everything we'd talked about in the weeks before I left. There was something deeply compassionate in his doing that. Today I'm drinking water that has been enhanced by the basil and the mint that we've got growing out front. It feels like a gift.

I force myself toward little pleasures - like beautiful and delicious water - to help balance the sadness I feel over my mother's death and the dawning reality of her being gone.

In Mary-Frances O'Connor's *The Grieving Brain*, she talks about the way the brain maps changes in life. When we're born, the brain maps the new landscape

. . . who picks us up when we cry, who feeds us, whose face it is that meets our little faces. And when someone core to our life dies, the brain needs to map that as well. To map that they are not here anymore. The empty space that is new in the landscape. Personally, I think that if we were not cushioned from the shock of such a death by this brain mapping, we might die ourselves or go mad.

I think it helps us in the mapping of the new landscape to try new little things to meet ourselves there. Things like beautiful and delicious water. It's pretty much all I can manage right now.

And it's enough to meet the moment.

Solstice Morning

The day is exquisite, soft and filled with bird song.

I'm stunned by the silence, when usually the sounds of car engines and lawn power tools punctuate the early part of the day.

I look around at the chaos in my space – my apartment strewn with Amazon boxes and things I've brought home from Mom's, things I haven't tidied in the normal course of days. There's also chaos in my inner space, as my brain maps a landscape without the usual markers that tell me I'm home, safe, and nourished.

It's ironic that the summer solstice in the northern hemisphere shifts into being when the sun crosses the zero degree of Cancer, the sign of the mother, and I am learning what it means to be without mine. I think about her so much, how much she loved life, how much she loved her family, how much she loved her home, how much she loved me.

How much she loved.

Someone once wrote that grief is the price we pay for love. I'm not sure I would say it quite that way, but I certainly feel what he or she was trying to communicate.

I spent some time this morning, in my morning journal, thinking about what my mother valued, what shaped her life. I came up with a list. I'm not sure it's exhaustive and I wonder why I chose what I chose to see today.

Here's a glimpse:

A beautiful home. Lovingly prepared meals. Travel and adventures. Laughter. Enjoyment. Art and Culture. Knowing where we come from.

Duty. Service. Family. Pleasure. Moderation. Caution. Country and citizenship. Having nice things. Later in life, she became more measured around money and spending. Responsibility.

There must be more. What am I missing? Why are these the things I see today?

A lone pickup truck guns its engine, drives off, and the street is quiet again.

Except for birdsong.

Kitchen Table Philosophy

Some nice bread and cheese.

A glass of cool water, infused with lemon and basil.

Birdsong.

Sunshine.

A breeze.

We choose what we see, the story we tell.

Mass shootings.

Politicians run amok.

A billionaire class that would starve the rest of the world.

Divisions among people.

Rape of the Earth.

All of this is there as well, existing in the same moment.

We choose what we see, the story we tell.

Some nice bread and cheese.

A glass of cool water, infused with lemon and basil.

Birdsong.

Sunshine.

A breeze.

The Art Waits

I stacked five pieces of art from my mother's house in the back of my car yesterday morning.

Later that afternoon, they were stacked in my son's living room. One leaned against the wall, the others rested on a table, white sheets of spongy paper between them on top of the glass. I sighed as I saw them there, while my brain organized this new information.

It's part of dismantling my mother's house, her home. The house will remain intact. The things that made it particularly hers, and a home, is what we're dismantling.

My place looks similar – with stacks of artwork leaning against walls, waiting. Waiting for how they will come together in my home. Similar stacks of art wait in my brothers' homes as well. There are pieces my daughter will take, my nephews, and others who we're not yet imagining.

The art waits, some of it still hanging on the walls in my mother's house.

She had a lot of art.

I don't know how she did it, put so much art on so few walls and made it look good.

But she had an eye for beauty. For pattern. For placement.

I can't get the image of stacked art, waiting, out of my mind. Like seeds carried by birds and planted in new places to flower in another bit of land. The tree hangs heavy with fruit that falls to the ground, seeds are planted, and life renews itself.

Fish for Breakfast

I'm restless this morning.

All I see are open projects, things left undone, papers that need to be collected and recycled, things out of place, things that have no place yet.

A coal seam in the landscape of my home.

I look around and feel bewildered. Where do I begin? It seems that *this* needs to happen before *that* can be done, and *that* needs to happen before *something else* can be done. Layers upon layers of things calling for my attention.

My attention feels like a limited resource these days. And I'm not sure that there's enough of it even on a good day to begin to clear things.

So, they sink, dead and decaying organic matter that falls into shallow and stagnant waters. Buried. The temperature increases and the pressure becomes greater. The compression and heat turn it into something harder, and harder still.

Carbon? Diamond?

Sometimes I open my fridge and look inside when my thoughts feel too big. I notice the fish I took out of the freezer last night to thaw for dinner tonight. The two small glass jars with stewed veg and sautéed veg that looked good, but that I had no idea what to do with when I moved them from freezer to fridge. I'd cooked it just before the unexpected trip to see my mother in the hospital.

The oven is preheating, and the Mahi-mahi is seasoned with olive oil, salt, and pepper in my cast iron skillet. The jars of veg sit on the counter. I'll add them when the fish is nearly done, heat everything together and combine the flavors.

My tea has gone cold while I've been writing.

The skillet goes into the oven, and I set the timer I brought home from Mom's. It was a gift from my daughter to her grandmother. It looks like a chubby blue bird with big eyes and yellow feet. My daughter said, "Please take this home with you, Mom. I like thinking about you using it and it being in your kitchen now." She told me to take other things too. A set of beautiful, hand-painted measuring bowls, a small plate with a beautiful quotation.

What has heart and meaning will find its way in. In the meantime, there's fish for breakfast.

40 Days

The morning has been quiet.

And the minute I pause before typing, a lawnmower next door begins to sing a discordant note against the morning's peace. I continue to type and it continues its relentless movement, it becomes part of the soundscape. There's a sense that what I expect, what I hope for, becomes replaced by something else, something not quite so welcome.

It's been 40 days since my mother's death, 40 days of walking through the wilderness of grief. A new landscape I would not have chosen to explore, but one that is mine nevertheless, a peaceful early morning interrupted by the sounds of power tools.

I think of Elijah asleep at the edge of the wilderness. He is exhausted, emptied by grief and trepidation about the future. He's lost his determination. His sense of self. His sense of knowing.

His sense of connectedness.

He wakes briefly. An angel is there with him. A cake is being cooked over a fire. It carries the fragrance of presence and nourishment. There is a jar of water.

Eat. Drink. You will need your strength for the journey ahead.

It will be 40 days of crossing an inhospitable landscape, one that a rare person would choose. But it is the only way to Horeb, the mountain of God. There are times in life when only God's companionship and counsel will do. This is one of those times.

It is a solitary journey, the only companionship a belly full of grace and a journey cloak of memory. An angel weaved it with words, water, and journey cake.

Finally reaching the mountain, climbing, climbing. Hiding in a dip in the rock, the only shelter from the elements. Fire, wind, earthquake.

Silence.

A voice calls his name.

Why are you here? Come out. Feel my embrace.

Remember who you are and that you have things to do.

He stands, wraps his mantle around his bony frame, and steps into the very power, presence, and palpability of God. There, on the precipice, more vulnerable than he's ever been before, he finds his footing. Begins to walk. Climbs down and moves forward, back across the landscape. Differently.

What has changed for him?

As I think about it today, I'm thinking that the beginnings of grief are a deep sense of aloneness. The movement through the landscape is discovery around presence. But there's also a sense that the awareness of being alone is true as well. Deeply true. And yet, there's also a sense of companioning that we put on like clothing. It's available to us but separate from us. And as we continue to live into this new thing, we get used to it. It becomes what now is real.

Again, I Cut Flowers in My Mother's Garden

Things are very different than the last time I wrote about this.

I'd come down to Washington to get away from things and find some quiet. The rest of my family had taken off for vacations to points north and west. My mother was alive. She was traveling as well. So, I was here and everyone else was gone. I'd come to do some writing, that year's counterpart to this writing project. I may also have been finalizing some things for the poetry collection that was published a year later.

Well, maybe some things are the same.

I've been invited to contribute to an anthology, so I'm creating a mini collection. I've got some poetry that I've been wanting to see if I can connect around a loose theme. It will be an interesting challenge to capture my mind.

Of course, even though many things are the same, everything is different.

But I've arrived. Evening has fallen and while the late afternoon light touched the garden, I cut some of the hydrangea bloom I've been eagerly anticipating. It will be the last year. Most of what is coming this year will be firsts, but this will be the last blossoming of this garden I will enjoy.

Cultivating Beauty in Gardens of Stone

I spent time again in my mother's garden today, cutting flowers.

I made bouquets and took them to the graves.

I've taken a week off for some bereavement time and am spending it away, at my mother's house. I hope for a quiet week, to let down and to be in grief without having to compartmentalize it in order to fulfil social and professional functions.

I woke up this morning with a migraine.

I'm not surprised, really. I've been holding a lot of tension in my body, and the freedom of rest enables it to release very quickly. Or maybe my body just doesn't know what to do with the energy when I no longer must hold it so tightly.

I've been moving gently through the day. I let myself cry when the impulse comes.

I took my time cutting flowers from all the hydrangea bushes in the garden - blue, deep purple, rich, deep pink, soft pink, and light, bright pink. The bouquet felt abundant and enormous as I carried it to the car. I cut some trailing vines from two of Mom's houseplants and dug out some gold cord from a bin that has gift wrapping supplies. A trimmed plastic water bottle held the flowers while I transported them.

The ride across town to the cemetery was slow, owing to heavy traffic. That's probably a good thing since Washington has installed traffic cameras everywhere to penalize careless or mildly distracted drivers.

The flowers from my aunt's burial almost three weeks ago were still there and directed me to her grave. I noticed a statue of an angel nearby, a landmark I'll use until the stone is placed. The ancestral plot is easy to find and well-marked. It's been almost 20 years since a grave has been opened there. The grass on Mom's grave has almost grown back completely. The new grass is the only thing that whispers that a grave was recently opened.

I made four bouquets with the flowers I brought and visited my grandparents, great-grandparents, aunt, and parents. I lingered with Mom for a while, wondering what enables us to leave the remains of those we love in the earth. It is an ancient practice that
hopes for rebirth – the tomb is a womb of sorts.

I'm not sure that we are deeply conscious of the ancient impulse.

To plant our parents like seeds in gardens of stone.

How to Be an Artist... Where it Began

Wendy Coad

Small town, big ideas. I knew what a big city was like because I'd run away to one at 17 with my boyfriend. Well, not actually run away, my mom and step-dad saw me off at the train-station. Mom was crying and telling me not to go and if I did go, not to expect anything, like a meager inheritance in 50 years. I think she was trying to dissuade me, but you can't do that to a 17-year-old, in love with the lead singer and bass guitarist in the local rock band. I was leaving, but pretended that I was going on my own. My step-father quietly handed me a note to read on the train. In it he said that he understood because he'd had left home at 13, and that if I ever needed anything to let them know. He was a very nice man. My grandmother had given me a bar of chocolate when I went to say goodbye. She didn't have anything else in the house she said, but she wanted me to have something for the trip. It was old and partially eaten and when I went to snack on the train, I saw it had tiny worms in it, so I threw it away.

    I was gone a year. It was before doing anything else, travel, college, so I guess you could call it my gap year. It was so exciting to be grown up. In fact, I'd felt grown up for a very long time, and believe I peaked in intelligence and wisdom at 15. I was so smart then and knew everything, more than I've ever known since. We set up house in a one-room rental in the area of Toronto called Chinatown. The room was so dirty that I washed all the walls and floor and then I moved on to degrease and scour the shared kitchen and bath. After that we moved in with a newly "citizenized" family just a few blocks away, occupying the top floor of their modest house. There was no door separating the floors, but we helped pay the rent on their new life and they mostly kept their children away.

    The big telephone conglomerate Ma Bell was where I got my first job as an operator. Directory assistance, I said every 17 seconds on average for 40 hours a week. Phones were still firmly attached to the wall then and assistance was cheerfully free. My supervisor told me that when she started there all the girls had to wear hat and gloves going to work, they owned you from your door to theirs. It was a bit surreal, but I took my job seriously because it was paying the rent, which was helping to pay for a new life for a family of 4. If you counted my boyfriend, then 6 of us were benefiting. Occasionally, out of boredom, I would answer the phone, "winter wonderland", with the same staccato that I said "directory assistance". No one seemed to notice and my fingers would deftly separate the pages of the huge volumes of names and businesses. In my whole life that was my only corporate job. Lucky, wasn't I?

I thought it was eternal love, but my boyfriend was philandering, he was tall, sturdy, rock band material. He told me if I thought I would ever regret not going to university that I should go. I thought about it and then I took the train back home. Promises were made but never kept. I was a bit of a romantic, but at 17, now 18, there was plenty yet ahead of me.

My mother cried, again, when I got home. She even said that she wasn't going to ask if she could see my arms. I had no idea what she was talking about, and then I realized she thought I had to leave because I was on drugs. Why else would you leave home, ever? Oh mom. Some families have answers to questions they can't explain or can't understand. The worst possible reason to stray from the fold was because you were under an influence so dark and so evil, you simply could not let go. One day this prophecy came true in our family, to our family, but not to me. That's someone else's story to tell, but not by me.

WINGS

Ethiopia 2018, Quilts for Kids, and the Beggar Lady

Terri Tomoff

In traveling to a truly foreign place, we inevitably travel to moods, states of mind, and hidden inward passages that we'd otherwise seldom have cause to visit. Pico Iyer

Travel: Why do we do it? Is it for pleasure? Work? A Bucket List Item? Immersing in the culture (s)? Or how about Therapy?

I want to think I travel for all those reasons except work. I never had a job requiring me to travel, except when I worked for the State of Ohio. Many training sessions were held in Columbus, so I motored down from Cleveland on I-71 to attend those "mandatory sessions," which was the extent of my work travel and never more than a day or two.

Over the last several decades, the travel bug has become my go-to therapy. I love to immerse myself in the different cultures around the block or, more aptly, around the world (I like going to less traveled places). The whole idea of planning, packing, and then flying to far-flung places on this great Earth brings me great pleasure. For me, though, it really doesn't matter if that travel consists of a loop around the block, a jaunt to the local grocery store, or, say, to someplace international, like Ethiopia. I'm all in on travel no matter where I am going, but I am incredibly giddy once I press the button for a plane ticket for that "big" trip somewhere exciting.

In 2018, I was fortunate to travel with my son's pediatric oncologist to Addis Ababa, Ethiopia (my son is a five-time cancer survivor - another story!). Not only did I see how this unbelievable doctor is motivated to save young children's lives who are diagnosed with cancer in a developing nation, but I was able to travel with her to meet the kids and families, visit the hospital where they are treated, and bring with me 35 quilts to donate to the then-named Mother Teresa Home, one for each bed. I am grateful that my small but mighty quilt guild has a philanthropic mindset and was gracious in providing brightly colored bed quilts to previous drab surroundings. Packing and schlepping them halfway across the world was no small feat, but the kids and staff appreciated it more than I could ever imagined.

After visiting the capital city of Addis Ababa for four days and hanging out with the cancer kids for some time while there, I continued traveling solo throughout this great country to other points of interest for the next week - Lalibela (home to the 11 rock-hewn churches) and Axum, on the Eritrea border. This travel was all before the civil wars in that particular area (north), and thankfully, I was safe my entire trip.

Immersing myself in the culture of 130,000,000 Ethiopians was genuinely amazing. From the bells ringing from the orthodox churches—a call to prayer for the believers, the garbage heaped on the streets (not so good), and the excellent hospitality I experienced everywhere I went, I couldn't get enough of the culture. There were so many differences from their world to the world I am used to, which made me pause on my own life. A resounding cacophony of thoughts about where I live, the food I eat, and the advantages and freedoms I get to enjoy each day were never lost on me.

Once I reached Lalibela, surprises and awe-inspiring moments were everywhere, for example, my hay mattress and pillow. But this is the scene in my travel story that quickly got my hackles up.

While sitting and eating my lunch on the outdoor patio area at my hotel, an Ethiopian meal *(An injera meal could include Kitfo (Traditional Marinated Minced Meat (that can sometimes be eaten raw), Shiro (Stew made from Ground Pulses), Kei Wot (Ethiopian Style Beef Stew), Gomen (Collard Greens), Kik Alicha (Yellow Split Pea Curry), Kei Tibs (Stir Fried Beef), Tibs (Spicy Beef Stew), and Kei Sir (Red Roots*) an "older" woman stopped by once she saw me sitting alone.

Other kids passed by me and asked for money, but I pointed for them to keep moving. Even though I did not understand their native tongue - Amharic - I figured out what they wanted from me. Within moments of the kids leaving the patio stoop looking for someone else to beg from, the older woman started to talk to me every so softly, all in Amharic. She had her hands on her hips and was getting louder with her harrumphs to gain my attention.

Without looking up from my meal or the maps spread out on my table, never acknowledging her, I detected her body language shifting out of the corner of my eye; she was about to start begging.

Gratefully, I was not alone on the patio with throngs of church coming and going passersby. There were also two tables of three men each on the patio. One table was comprised of men over 30 or 40 years old, and the other table was comprised of younger men under 21 or so. They were busy chatting to themselves and never paid me any mind. I was thrilled to sit down, eat a great meal, and spread my maps of the area until my guide picked me back up for our afternoon rock-hewn church tour.

By the way, my guide and others who knew my travel plans to the area all suggested that I ignore all pleas and not look the beggars in the eye or offer them anything. Ever.

As I continued to eat and ignore her, the lady beggar raised her voice to me. With each utterance and tsk tsk, I could feel her dark eyes drilling into the side of my downward face. It didn't seem like she would give up on me so soon after her steadily loud, annoying pleadings. Her begging went on for several minutes. I started sweating. I had no idea how to handle this situation, and I knew I couldn't give her a thing, even though I thought about it for a nanosecond.

Then, without "warning," she began screaming (or was it screeching?) at me. As hard as it was, I held my head down and continued to eat my food without looking up. My face had to be beet red by then. Her full-blown tirade made me more uncomfortable, though I used every ounce of energy to keep calm under pressure, kept my head down, and did not look up. I wondered where the heck the manager on duty was to possibly quell this commotion on the patio and hopefully "shoo" her away. If in earshot, he had to hear the screeching. I couldn't do the shoo-ing away. For a few moments, I strained my eyes on the periphery, though I did not raise my head to see if any of the six men on the patio would help me or escort the beggar lady away.

No such luck at that point.

The old beggar lady and I were in a battle of wills. She screamed at me, and I kept my head down so far I could have eaten my meal like a dog. When she raised her voice again, she continued screaming a few octaves higher. Once at the top of her lungs and not giving up, one young man got up from his table and walked over to the beggar lady. He gave her some coins (Birr) to move on, and she did.

Whew! Finally! The seven people on the patio were now relieved, but no one was more relieved than me. I was spent. I like to spread joy and kindness, and I couldn't do that.

That young man did that for me, but I secretly hoped it was for him and the other lunch patrons. I think he knew how upset I got; who wouldn't? As he walked by my table, I mouthed "Thank You" and bowed my head to his kindness. He nodded back to me, acknowledging our awkwardness during that lunch hour. I was so thankful he had stepped up to diffuse this mortifying situation because now, thinking back, it must have been written all over my face (if they could see it!).

Honestly, while on that lovely patio, I was a "sitting" duck and a prime target for the begging brigade. An hour later, my guide returned to pick me up for the rest of the day, and all was "forgotten."

Frozen and cringing during those crazy 10 minutes on the patio, I had to chalk it up as it was all part of travel. While revisiting this trip to write this travel essay, I do have to admit that I like these travel snafus way after the moment because they stretch me down to my core like no other.

Butterfly Wisdom

Katharina Hren

"I hate Costa Rica, I hate the rain forest, I hate you, I hate everyone, and I ESPECIALLY HATE YOGA!"

We were forging uphill in the blazing sun, a handful of sweaty parents and our shuffling along children, a motley crew on a family yoga retreat. I had missed the warning signs, namely Gustav's beet red cheeks, while we hiked to join a canopy zipline tour. My nine year old son had clearly reached some kind of limit.

Just the night before, the yoga teacher's two sons Alejandro and Juan, both more outgoing and older than my son at 11 and 13, had been bragging about all the times they had done the zipline tour in the past. While swept up in the boys' boisterous energy, my son decided he wanted to go. There were only four other children in the group – the three homeschooled mild-mannered and well-behaved children who always stuck together and the precocious 4 year old girl with the British accent. None of these kids were Gustav's age, and although he was used to entertaining himself as an only child, he seemed to be struggling to fit in.

I had been looking forward to hanging out with serious and committed yogis when I booked the trip, but the other two Moms in the group were not at all interested in talking about yogic philosophy or yoga poses. Amy, the homeschooling Mom who was married to a doctor, always seemed to face in the other direction when I sat next to her at dinner. Jennifer, the lawyer Mom, who had just left a fancy and important job in London, kept talking about her next yoga retreat, which was taking place the following week at a luxury resort on the other side of Costa Rica. She expressed her displeasure with the eco-friendly aspects of our retreat center, such as how it was solar-powered and there was no bar or pool.

That morning, at yet another extravagant and delicious breakfast of exotic fruit juices, eggs, and pancakes, under the watchful eye of an iguana, Gustav had changed his mind.

"I don't want to go any more," he said quietly.

His eyes were averted from the far side of the table where Maria's boys were once again telling stories about flying over the trees, loudly emphasizing how high the zipline was and laughing at the other children's reactions. Maria had just announced to the group that we would all be going on the hike to the zipline place whether we were ziplining or not.

The sun was much more intense than the Milwaukee summer sun we were used to, and since we were walking away from the ocean, it was starting to feel even hotter. We were halfway to the zipline adventure center when Gustav had his meltdown, raising his voice in a way that was alarming. My face started to turn its own unique shade of red. Our guide suggested giving Gustav some water, which seemed to calm him down, and someone else gave him a hat to wear. We were too far from the retreat center to turn back, and eventually my son seemed to accept his fate because he stopped complaining. He got quieter, but my anxiety was now on slow boil. This kid was used to a lot of walking while on vacation with me, but we had never been south of the equator before.

Once we got back into the shelter of the rainforest I distracted Gustav by telling him to look for monkeys.

"Do you see any monkeys?" I asked. "Try to look as high as you can. If you are patient, perhaps you will see a monkey head or tail…!"

The trees in the rainforest are so tall and dense that you really have to crane your neck to see any signs of movement. I was rather afraid that we might see snakes. Gustav had decided during another rainforest excursion that he was afraid of army ants. He even said that he hoped we would not die on this trip.

To be honest, I had not expected him to be afraid. He had been on airplanes since the age of 2. The previous year we were in Spain, and when he entered the sea for the first time, he would not leave for hours. When I briefly lost him in a train station during that same trip, he was flanked by two security guards when he confidently pointed me out to them. He loved animals and exploring nature – I thought for sure that he would thrive in Costa Rica.

Instead, I felt like the worst mother in the world as I realized my usually easygoing son had reached his edge. The previous day we had learned about a flower called "yesterday today and tomorrow" or "San Juan". In the past he had had a mother and father who lived together. His concept of today meant not seeing his dad very much. When I thought about his tomorrows, I could feel my heart beat faster under my tongue. By showing him more of the world, I was hoping to increase his confidence and teach him to honor his instincts.

During one of our rainforest walks we were delighted to learn that there is a kind of tree in the jungle that grows by moving over time, as though it actually walks. This felt like the perfect metaphor to guide my son through life. The zipline tour seemed like another way to help Gustav believe in himself. I wanted him to know that not only could he walk a steady path, but he could also fly!

After we finally got to the zipline center, we were cautioned that once it started, there was no turning back. I reminded Gustav that I was right behind him, every step of the way. I kept my fear of heights to myself so that he would not get even more scared. We had to climb a long ladder to get to the first platform and be strapped into the harness that was clipped to the zipline. I stifled the urge to laugh hysterically when we had to step onto a loose piece of wood the size of a telephone book. We had climbed so high up into the trees, and still there was another step to take. What if I stumbled on this block of wood, this high up on this platform? Parenthood seemed to offer plenty of opportunities to stumble.

One of the guides heard me speaking German to my son, my attempt to keep the others from hearing our conversation, and he told us that he was from Switzerland. I watched Gustav make it to the second platform, where he then announced that he could not continue. Panic set in. I was about to remind him that he could not stop. Did he not remember that they said we could not turn back? Seconds later I was incredulous as the Swiss guide in the middle of Costa Rica kindly told my son that it was ok, they would go back. Since he was 9, and I was 40, I did not think it would go over well if I screamed that I was only doing this to encourage him, and he should let me go back too.

Thirteen platforms. Twelve more to go. Still, since parenting seemed to involve flying by the seat of my pants, this seemed like some kind of initiation into the not so far off teen years.

Later I found Gustav curled up in a hammock. I was told that he had fallen asleep almost immediately, which reminded me of how we had each handled getting seasick differently. While sailing on a friend's boat in Lake Michigan, I had thrown up all over the side of the boat and could not wait to get back to shore. Gustav had curled up into a ball on the floor of the boat and slept peacefully for the entire journey. Perhaps his instincts were serving him better than I realized.

When the retreat ended, the people who had prepared and served the food, as well as cleaned our cabins, were the ones who accompanied me and Gustav to the boat we would take to the other side of the bay in order to get to the tiny airport in Drake Bay. Maria gave me a heart shaped stone that she found on the beach.

"Adios, Gustavo! Pura Vida!"

We had made some friends after all.

The lawyer Mom was quick to unfriend me on Facebook though.

After we returned home, my son told me his ideas for a butterfly discovery center. On our last day in San Jose, we had visited a butterfly farm. Gustav said that he would like to teach people about butterflies, especially the differences between butterflies and moths. I asked him if he thought people are more like butterflies or moths, and he said,

"Butterflies of course, which is why you need to teach butterfly yoga.

Yoga and meditation release the spiritual mind which is trapped in the body."

He did not seem to notice that my mouth had dropped open. None of the adults on our yoga retreat had shared these kinds of insights, not even the teacher. Gustav went on to tell me that butterflies have a lot to teach people about their own colors on the insides and transformation. He then told me about all the animal yoga poses he had been inventing. Perhaps the family yoga retreat had not been such a bad idea after all.

Dust Sandwiches & Olive Groves: Life Lessons from the Spanish Countryside

Amber Field

My junior year in college, I studied abroad in Seville, Spain. I was a Computer Science major who had nearly completed all of the Spanish Linguistics coursework as well. I kept taking Spanish courses for one reason only: I had a life goal of becoming fluent in a second language. After nine-and-a-half years of classroom Spanish, it became clear that I would never become fluent unless I spent significant time outside of the United States. That's how I ended up taking a break from my programming classes and studying in Spain for the semester.

The best part of the study abroad program was that I got to live with a Spanish family and their Spanish cats in a Spanish apartment, speaking only Spanish because they didn't speak any English whatsoever. *Mi familia* was a mother, Concha, and her 35-year-old daughter, Lola. Concha's husband died many years before, and they made ends meet through a variety of odd jobs as well as by hosting foreign exchange students like me. In Spain, an unmarried 35-year-old living at home is normal. High prices and close family ties mean that kids live at home much longer than in the United States. It was Lola who introduced me to Spanish music, found me a good internet café, and tried in vain to teach me how to walk on cobblestones in impossibly high heels.

We lived in a second-floor apartment in the Triana neighborhood, directly above a *carnicería* (butcher shop) and down the street from a *panadería* (bakery), a *frutería* (fruit store), and a whole host of other delightful specialty shops. Each day, Concha would walk down our street and gather the ingredients for our breakfast (always toast with copious amounts of olive oil poured on top) and the mid-day meal.

Concha made amazing Spanish food. When she made her version of Spain's famous egg and potato dish, *tortilla española*, she always made an entire tortilla - a whole frying pan full - just for me. She gave me a few recipes, from memory, at the end of the semester, which I diligently wrote down on scraps of paper. Though they are filled with vague quantities and sometimes hard-to-find ingredients, I am thankful to have these loose connections to my Spanish culinary experience to this day. The recipes take me right back to that tiny apartment kitchen in Triana.

The neighborhood had very little green space, but we had a balcony that was covered in plants. Amongst them sat a small cardboard box kept specifically for their very large cat, Gordito, who loved to sit in it and make the sides bow outward with his girth. I loved every minute I spent at home with *mi familia*, but I also found plenty of time to explore the rest of Spain.

My classes were set-up such that I had a four-day weekend each week, which I used to travel all over Spain, Portugal, and Italy. I was gone nearly every weekend, off with different groups of newly made friends to explore the country. Concha would always ask me if I'd like a sandwich of some sort to take with me on the train and I would name one. One week I asked for a *sandwich de polvo* – a turkey sandwich. Instead of promising to make me one, both Concha and Lola laughed and laughed at me. "Are you sure you want a 'polvo sandwich'?" they said. "*Sí, sí, por supuesto* (yes, of course)," I responded. Until I realized that turkey was actually *pavo* and I'd ordered a "dust sandwich". They were a good, kind family and I got along with them really well.

But, despite making a lot of friends through the program, I often felt lonely that semester. Spanish culture is full of extroverts who like to stay out late. By contrast, I typically enjoy a good one-on-one conversation and an early run. Other students' families wrote them letters and came to visit. My mom was diagnosed with multiple sclerosis that October. I found out over the telephone standing in an empty alley near my apartment, and my parents were never able to visit. I missed my own friends, my family, my ability to communicate fluently, and free public bathrooms that actually supplied toilet paper.

One week, Concha came to me and said, "We don't normally take our students on trips, but this Saturday we'd like to take you on a day trip". It was perfect timing as I hadn't made any travel plans yet. All she told me was that we'd be going to the Spanish countryside a couple hours outside of town. I never did learn exactly where we went.

We drove and drove–through fields and farms, pastures, and small towns. Past the iconic bull-shaped billboards advertising Osborne Brandy and the windmills made famous by Cervantes in Don Quixote.

Suddenly, we stopped in the middle of nowhere on a gorgeous hillside, and I was told to get out of the car. We were the only ones around for miles.

That's when I started to panic a little. Wait, just me? Where are we? Maybe Concha and Lola didn't actually like me after all. This would be the perfect place to leave an annoying American student and never look back.

They got out with me. (Ok, phew!) We parked the car on a dirt road leading farther up the hill, right next to the cutest stone fence you've ever seen. And though Concha was 65 and I've never seen her workout beyond the walks she takes around the neighborhood every day, she hoofed it up the hill ahead of us! Eventually, we arrived at a beautiful grove of olive trees. "This is my orchard," she said. "I've been growing these trees for years, and each year, I pay a friend to turn these olives into olive oil, and we sell the oil in town." How very Spanish of them.

The trees looked ready, she said. So we walked back down to the car and drove into a tiny town, stopping at an old, sprawling residence. It had an oversized entryway for the horses of days gone by, a courtyard, and large rooms with tile flooring. We walked right in. This, it turned out, was where their extended family lived, and I got to meet every single one of them.

One of the things I loved best about living in Southern Spain was that as the temperature got colder, they had no tolerance for it whatsoever. As a light chill settled over the country, they brought out their space heaters and giant, heavy tablecloths. We'd gather around a table in the living room with our legs under the tablecloth while the space heater churned out beautiful radiant warmth from underneath.

In this spacious country living room, they had a TV but not much else of modern convenience. Their version of the space heater experience was a giant dining table with an actual fire built underneath in the center of it and that same giant, thick tablecloth helping us stay warm in the fall breeze. They left the door and the windows open, which made the room feel like an Icelandic thermal bath: warm underneath and wonderfully breezy on top. We huddled around conversing with the show *Los Simpson* playing, dubbed in Spanish, in the background. I learned all about their lives–their family tree, what animals they were raising, funny stories I wish I'd written down about Concha, and jokes about how *Los Simpson* doesn't make sense. I guess they had *The Simpsons* on just for me, and that show is just too culturally tied to the United States to translate properly. I cherished the time I was there, and as I sat there listening, that loneliness which had always been hiding deep down under the surface that semester lifted away. My heart was full.

Then something important occurred to me. I'd achieved my goal of becoming fluent in Spanish. There is no way I could have sat and talked with a Spanish family for hours, laughing at their jokes, and enjoying their stories if I hadn't hit this momentous milestone. But that wasn't the most important thing I'd done in Spain. This car ride, this hike, this amazing time that I got to spend with my extended Spanish family, was the most quintessentially Spanish thing I'd done all semester. It didn't matter how many cities in Spain I'd been to, how many flamenco shows I saw, cathedrals I toured, classes in Spanish I took, or massive public parks I sat in. This, right here, was Spain. The people, the connection with your roots, and the olive trees swaying in the breeze of the beautiful countryside. I'd immersed myself in the essence of Spain and accepted a completely new culture. And that culture accepted me.

A Spanish Family Trip

Maggie Ford Croushore

THE DECISION

Reading on the couch after the kids had gone to sleep, my husband walked into the room.

Smiling, phone in his hand, he sat down next to me. "I just talked to my mom. My cousin set a date for his wedding. Guess where it's going to be?"

I looked up from my book, pausing to think. "Ireland?"

His cousin was Irish and had been engaged for a while. We had always said that whenever he got married, we should try to go. We had been wanting to take a trip to Ireland for some time and this felt like a great opportunity.

My husband smiled. "No." He paused. "Spain. Outside of Barcelona."

He let it sink in. I squealed. "Spain?! That's amazing. When?"

I lived and studied for a semester in college in Sevilla, in southern Spain, and have been wanting to go back there ever since. My husband knew my adoration for the country and had heard many, many stories.

"Next year. Basically, on your birthday."

"We have to go," I said without even thinking.

He responded. "I do think we should seriously consider it. I might be the only one invited to the actual wedding, though, since they are keeping it really small."

"I don't care. I can work with that. I'll see your cousins and family during the day and over that weekend. I have to go." I paused and smiled. "You can't go to Spain without me, especially on my birthday."

He smiled back. "I'm aware."

The rest of the evening was filled with Google searches for traveling in Spain with kids--what to do, what to expect, what to avoid, what to pack, where to stay, travel car seats, and on and on. While I had once lived there, that was nearly 18 years ago and I didn't have kids at the time. This would be a very different experience.

It didn't take too long to figure out the logistical pieces of planning an international trip as a family of five. That was the "easy" part. The harder part of the decision was thinking through whether or not we could handle it. My daughter was born six weeks after the coronavirus pandemic shut the world down, so we had spent the first couple years of her life mostly at home. We hadn't traveled much as a family of five and had never been on an airplane all together. Even going to restaurants often ended in disaster; we mapped out our exit strategy before we ordered drinks. Causing scenes across Spain, a place I held so dearly in my heart, struck me with fear.

To gauge how ready we were for an international trip, we purposefully went to a "nicer" Spanish restaurant to "practice" eating tapas. I had been wanting to go to this particular restaurant for months and this seemed like the perfect opportunity to try it. We decided to go early on a Saturday evening, around 5pm, figuring we could get a table, eat, and finish dinner before the real dinner rush began. When we arrived, the restaurant was mostly empty. We got a table in the corner near the bathrooms right away.

Perfect. Far away from other people. Easy exit to the bathroom.

As we made our way to the table, the server asked if we needed a highchair for any of our kids. I looked at my husband. He shrugged.

I turned to the server. "Sure. One highchair would be great." Carrying my three-year-old daughter on my hip, I looked her in the eyes. "You want to sit in a really cool chair?"

Without saying a word she turned her head aggressively into my shoulder, nearly knocking me over. The server walked to the table with the highchair in her hands and looked at me with questioning eyes.

I glanced at my husband and slightly rolled my eyes before turning to the server and smiling. "Thank you. You can just put the chair at the end of the table." I turned to my husband and said, under my breath, "It'll be fine. We'll figure it out."

We were all standing around the table surrounded by four regular chairs and one highchair, my husband and I at opposite sides of the table. My eight-year-old son raced to the seat next to my husband, pushing his brother to the side in the process. "I call the seat next to Dad!"

My five-year-old son immediately started to cry. "Not fair! I wanted to sit next to Daddy!"

Still on my hip, my daughter chimed in "Not me! I want Mommy's lap!" She tightened her grasp on me.

All three children began whining, crying, and talking at once. My eyes met my husband's. "Well, this is off to a great start."

"Sure is." He half smiled.

I transformed into Mommy fix-it mode. I calmed down my five-year-old by giving him a hug and bringing out some crayons and a coloring book from my backpack, placing them in front of the chair next to me. I convinced him that he actually really wanted to sit next to me the whole time, since he would likely want to be next to me in the next ten minutes anyway. My older son settled in next to my husband while my daughter sat on my lap.

I exhaled.

We can do this. It will be great. Everything's fine.

We had around ninety seconds of calm, enough time for my husband and I to speed read the menu, rattling off various tapas that appealed to us and would at least be somewhat appetizing to our children. The server came over carrying glasses of water for the table. Approximately three seconds after she put the glasses on the table, my five-year-old turned to show me his coloring book and knocked his water over completely, soaking his shirt and my pants in the process. He stopped short and I knew I had about five seconds before he either lost it or was okay. Without thinking, I stood up, gently took his hand and started walking to the bathroom to clean him up. My daughter was still sitting on my lap. I attempted to place her in the highchair. She tightened her legs, kicking them around my waist and stiffening up so that there would be no physical possibility of getting her into it. I sighed and adjusted her back on my hip. I looked at my husband, who had grabbed a napkin to clean the spill. My eight-year-old was reading the menu, seemingly unaware of what was going on. "I am going to take them to the bathroom to get dry. You can order what we just talked about."

My husband nodded. "Sounds good. Good luck."

I smiled and widened my eyes. "Thanks."

It's still fine. Everything is fine. We will make it through dinner.

After getting my son and I somewhat dry, we made it back to the table. Our bread had just arrived.

My three and five-year-old gasped in delight and exclaimed, in unison, "Bread!"

I met their energy. "Yay! Bread. Your favorite."

My daughter corrected me. "My *favorite* favorite, Mommy!"

I gave her a hug. "That's right. Bread is your *favorite* favorite." My five-year-old had already taken a giant bite out of a piece of bread sitting on his plate.

Before I sat down, I tried again to see if my daughter wanted the highchair, so I could sit by myself. "You want to sit in your special chair?"

She lunged for the bread, nearly falling out of my arms. "No, Mommy. I'll sit on your lap."

I smiled, not surprised with her choice. I paused for a moment, considering if I should try to convince her otherwise. But I knew that was a losing argument. I looked at the table. I saw some Sangria in a glass. I looked at my husband. "Sangria? Gracias, amor."

He smiled back. "De nada."

We got through the rest of our meal without too much incident. My husband and eight-year-old ended up getting in an (age-appropriate) discussion about the Spanish Civil War, my five-year-old discovered his love of all things jamón ibérico, and my three-year-old remained firmly on my lap.

All in all, it could have been far worse. As we left the restaurant, my mind raced.

Can the kids handle a trip to Spain?

Can I handle a trip to Spain with three young kiddos?

On the drive home, I turned to my husband. "Well, that wasn't great, but I still think we should do it." I paused. "We should go to Spain."

He took my hand, eyes on the road ahead, laughing. "Let's talk tonight." Then, he glanced at me quickly. "But I agree. We should do it."

So, after weeks of incessant Googling and a somewhat failed "practice" tapas experience, we made the decision deep down we knew we would make all along: in roughly 5 months, we were going to Spain.

It'll be fine.

It'll be great.

It'll be.

LA PRINCESA

After two long, mostly uneventful flights with minimal vomit, we were finally in Barcelona and ready for our first night in Spain. Arriving in Barcelona was a pinch myself moment. It had been nearly 18 years since I was last in Spain and I had been wanting, waiting and wishing to come back ever since.

On the drive to our apartment, my children bounced in their seats, their sparkling eyes filled with wonder as they looked out the window at the "really cool" buildings and listened to me speaking in my limited Spanish with our cab driver.

In the middle of asking the driver for a recommendation for a place to find the best tapas near where we were staying, my daughter gasped. "Mama!"

My son chimed in, "You are speaking Spanish, Mommy. Spanish! I didn't know you could talk like that."

I laughed. "Yes, Mommy does speak some Spanish and our driver is being very patient with me when I don't remember words. It's fun to speak Spanish, especially…" I paused. "...in Spain! Do you want to learn more Spanish?"

They nodded emphatically while smiling ear-to-ear.

"Fantástico."

They giggled and returned to gazing out their windows at the stunning vistas.

When we arrived at our apartment, I wanted to go straight to bed but knew that assimilating to the new time zone as quickly as possible was the best way to combat jet lag. Besides that, while my exhaustion was fierce, my desire to explore Barcelona with my family was even fiercer.

We wandered to a nearby mall that used to be a bullfighting arena to get some dinner on the rooftop. Coming off the elevator, the view took my breath away. We could see the entire city. We walked a few laps around, gazing at the view and taking some pictures, before finding a restaurant serving dinner. The place was adorable with a table outside, a delicious sounding menu with traditional Spanish tapas and, most importantly, the ability to seat us right away. My dream of a perfect first night in Spain seemed within reach.

My dream was interrupted, however, when my brain flashed to our failed tapas dinner five months prior and several other attempts in the meantime. My heart rate increased as we made our way to the table. I could see that the crankiness and exhaustion was catching up to them. It was catching up to me too. The last thing I wanted was to cause a scene. Before we even sat down, they were already arguing over who was going to sit where and have what cup even though all of the cups on the table were identical.

Well, this is not off to a great start.

The sweat began to form and my visions of a fun family Spanish dinner were replaced by visions of everything spilling, children throwing food, and at least one of my children under the table screaming. It had all happened before, most recently at the airport when my daughter spent a good ten minutes under the table because she didn't like the straw she got with her apple juice.

Just breathe. It will be fine. Stay calm.

I took some deep breaths. I opened my mouth to spring into Mommy fix-it mode when the server appeared with a highchair, presumably for my three-year-old daughter. I started to say, in my limited Spanish, that she wouldn't need the highchair.

However, before I could muster anything, I was stopped in my tracks.

This MVP of a server didn't just bring the chair. He presented it, bowing his head, placing it before my daughter and elegantly saying, "Para la princesa..."

I held my breath, looking at my daughter. I looked at my husband whose expression matched mine.

She looked at the server, widening her eyes in delight. She was speechless--a rare occurrence. Without saying a word, she smiled ear-to-ear while she placed her hand to her chest as if to say, "Who, me?!" She nodded slightly while demurely looking to the side. The server placed the chair at the end of the table. She eagerly climbed in.

I exhaled and blinked several times.

Did that actually just happen? Did she willfully sit in a highchair? And smile about it?

The rest of the meal was dreamy.

We ordered rounds and rounds of tapas and each of my children tried at least a bite of each. My three and five-year-old decided that they loved pan, agua, and tortilla española. My eight-year-old tried octopus and decided that it was now his favorite food. He also asked a million questions about Spain and Barcelona and Sevilla and rattled off the stats of all of his favorite

Spanish soccer players. They all drank from crystal-like glasses. Nothing spilled. Nothing broke. They politely requested more tapas and actually ate them when they arrived.

As a family, we talked, laughed, ate, and enjoyed a leisurely meal of nearly 2 hours. It was a far cry from our last meal at the airport where at least one person, myself included, had had tears at one point or another. In fact, it was a far cry from any other meal we had ever had at a restaurant. My daughter sat in her princesa chair the ENTIRE meal.

As we were leaving the restaurant, my daughter hugged her princesa chair and the server. My boys practiced their Flamenco moves, which I had described and demonstrated earlier in the evening. We were going to see a Flamenco show in Sevilla and they wanted to be prepared.

It all felt so foreign. So…Spanish.

Thank you, Spain. I think we are going to have a great trip.

SEVILLA

Holding my breath with each tight turn that miraculously didn't end in a crash, I sat in awe. Our driver navigated the narrow streets like the absolute professional he was while also talking to me about everything I had missed in Sevilla over the last eighteen years. The sights and sounds of Sevilla surrounded me with a warm embrace. I felt at home. And the fact that I was back in Sevilla with my husband and children felt like a dream come true.

There were so many things that I wanted to do in Sevilla. I had carefully planned each day, building in lots of time to walk around the city and explore, to ensure we experienced all of my favorite spots. The agenda included touring the historic Catedral de Sevilla where Christopher Colombus was buried, wandering around the palace with peacocks at the Real Alcázar de Sevilla, visiting Parque de María Luisa---one of my favorite parks of all time-- that featured a breathtaking fountain at the Plaza de España and miles of stunning orange trees, seeing a live Flamenco show, touring the Sevilla soccer stadium in my old neighborhood, and eating as many tapas as we could fit in our bellies.

Through it all, though, my unstated goal was to make my husband and three children fall in love with Sevilla, just like I did when I lived there for a semester in college.

By the end of our time there, I was proud to have achieved that goal.

On our last night in Sevilla, we decided to splurge on a nicer restaurant, getting reservations in advance and dressing in our fanciest outfits. My husband and I brought some distractions for the children, including the iPad, in case things took a turn. Our dinners had been quite smooth but we were not about to take any chances.

We sat down at the table, my daughter happily in her princesa chair, and ordered an obscene amount of tapas including our new favorites: octopus, jamón ibérico, tortilla española, patatas bravas, and copious amounts of bread and water. It was an absolute feast. In the middle of the meal, I decided it was time to do some family reflections--some highs from our time in Sevilla. I had the impression that everyone loved it, but I felt the need to hear it for myself, to further calm the voice that was still inside of me telling me that a trip to Spain with three young children was a little bananas.

I clinked a bread knife gently against my wine glass. My children and husband stopped their conversations and looked at me. "All right. You know what time it is?"

My daughter raised her hand, "My turn! I go first!"

This kind of reflection was a ritual at home so they knew what was coming. I laughed. "Of course, sweetie. You can go first. What was your high from Sevilla?"

She sat up in her seat, looking to the side and smiling wide. "Hmmm. My high was the Flamenco show!" She danced with her hands, pretending to be a Flamenco dancer. "And BREAD!" She held up her bread and pointed to her oldest brother to go next.

My eight-year-old looked to the side, deep in thought about his high before opening his mouth to speak. "I liked a lot of stuff but my high was probably the Cathedral and seeing the tomb of Christopher Colmbus. I mean, I can't believe that he is actually buried there." He kept talking about all that he learned during our tour. "Oh, and the tour of the soccer stadium. That was cool. And octopus. I love octopus." He chose his brother to go next.

"My high was…" my five-year-old looked around and grabbed some bread and jamón. "...pan! And also agua. And also I really like the cool playgrounds, climbing to the top of the tower and seeing the soccer stadium." He smiled and took another bite of his food, pointing at my husband.

My husband smiled and took a sip of his drink, thinking about his high. "It's hard to pick one, honestly. This place is like a fairy tale." He looked me in the eyes and took my hand from across the table. "I really do love it here."

Tears filled my eyes. "I know. Me too. Being here with you all is a dream come true."

We all talked for a few more minutes about the highlights of our time in Sevilla. We finished the meal and let the children watch a show on the iPad while my husband and I drank some wine and kept talking about how much we loved this magical place.

Goal achieved.

THE BAG THAT SAVED ME

Pulling up to the train station in Sevilla, I glanced at my watch.

Plenty of time.

I thanked the driver in Spanish, quickly unbuckled my children from their travel safety harnesses, and grabbed the suitcases the driver kindly took out of the trunk.

Today was a travel day, so my anxiety level was not low. We were all a bit sad to say goodbye to the city we all came to love so dearly, but knew that it was time to move on to our next adventure: back to Barcelona.

Boarding the train was chaotic, as expected, but we found our seats without too much trouble. The luggage racks in our train car were full by the time we got there, so my husband lugged our enormous suitcases two cars down while I got the kiddos set up with their tablets, snacks, coloring books, lovies, water bottles, and more. By the time he got back, we were settled. A couple hours later, the conductor called our stop, and my husband and I planned our exit strategy.

"I'm going to head to the other car in just a couple of minutes to grab our bags." He started.

"Makes sense to me. Avoid the crowds. I can have the kiddos ready to go and we can meet you on the platform." I paused. "Can you help get the kiddos ready now?"

"Of course."

We went into operation "de-screen" and "de-snack" the children. We were almost at our stop and everything was mostly organized. I looked at my husband. "Go. I got this. I'll see you on the platform."

"Great. Thanks, babe. It may take me longer than you."

I smiled. "We will see about that. You know that transitions can be a bit challenging for our crew."

He smiled back. "Good point."

He leaned over to give me a quick kiss before heading two cars down to retrieve our bags. I finished helping my kiddos get ready and got myself ready, too. I stood up to put on my backpack, filled with all of the essential supplies for our travels, and helped my daughter get her backpack on while sitting in the seat in front of me. I looked across the aisle.

"Hey boys. We are almost there. As you know, Daddy just went to get our bags and is going to meet us outside on the platform."

I paused, looking at my daughter in front of me and to the right at my boys. "Please get your backpacks on, just like me, so that we can get ready to get off the train when it is our turn."

I paused again to reiterate the plan. "Okay, what are we doing right now?"

My oldest son shouted, "Backpacks on!" The younger two chimed in, "Yeah. Backpacks!"

"Exactly! And then…?"

"Stay close to Mommy and get off the train when it's our turn!"

"Perfect! You are all incredible travelers!" I cheered.

The train jolted to a stop. I could feel my heart racing and the sweat beginning to form on my forehead.

It's okay. I got this. Backpacks are on. Kiddos are prepped. We only have to make it a short distance. Everything is great.

I plastered on an extra large smile to further prove that I was fine.

"All right, kiddos. This is it. Get ready. Our turn will be up soon."

People around us were standing and I saw folks several rows up starting to move. I took note of the people in front of us, mentally calculating when it would be our turn.

"Almost us. Backpacks on?" I looked across the aisle at my boys. "Great! We are ready to rock."

Then. THE COUGH...

Time stood still. Everything became slow motion as the vomit arrived. Lots and lots and lots of vomit.

Noooooo. No no no no. This cannot be happening. Not now.

Without thinking, I cupped my hands together and placed them under my daughter's mouth. I was just in time to catch the avalanche of vomit projecting from her adorable little face. Thankfully (?) most of the vomit landed in my hands and not on the seat, ground, or her.

I was frozen. Everything I needed was in my backpack, which *inconveniently* was on my back--barf bags, wipes, extra clothes, Dramamine, etc. Hands full of vomit, I was immobilized. I looked over at my boys. They covered their mouths with their hands. My oldest looked like he was about to be sick.

Can they somehow get into my backpack? No, no they cannot.

The entire train car collectively gasped. I saw looks of empathy and disgust.

Think. Think. THINK.

Like a gift from Above, an El Corte Inglés plastic bag appeared over my shoulder, thrown over the seat by the friendly 20-something couple sitting in front of me. I mustered a quick "Gracias. Muchas gracias."

Naturally, our section of the car began filing out of their seats at this exact moment. People poured into the aisle, gently holding their noses and giving me sympathetic glances.

With my new saving grace of a bag, I sprang into action. I gently tilted my cupped hands so that the vomit pooled on my daughter's green dress (her favorite dress, I might add). I carefully removed the dress, avoiding getting vomit all over her face and hair, and placed the dress in the plastic bag. In an impressive swoop, I hurled the backpack off my back, opened it, and gathered baby wipes, more plastic bags, and a barf bag for my daughter in case she got sick again. I quickly wiped the vomit off my daughter as best I could. To lighten the mood, I gave her many hugs and sang songs while I cleaned up.

My poor baby girl.

I looked at my boys, who were patiently waiting, standing and looking at the situation with a mixture of awe and horror. While it had only been a couple of minutes, the entire train car was empty.

"Thank you so much for waiting so patiently, boys. Let's get off this train and meet up with Daddy. He's probably wondering where we are!" I used a sing-song voice to lighten the mood.

They looked concerned but didn't ask questions.

Drenched in sweat and vomit, I carried my daughter while guiding my boys off the train. The moment we got off, I saw my husband with our big suitcases. He looked annoyed. However, when he saw my face--scrunched, sweaty and cartoon-angry--any annoyance turned to concern.

"Everything okay? I was starting to get worried…" He asked as I walked towards him and past him, not daring to stop.

"I know. We're fine. Everything's fine." I looked at my daughter. "She got sick, but it's fine now."

My tone and demeanor told a different story. My husband read between the lines.

"I'm sorry babe. That doesn't sound fun." He was now walking alongside me, suitcases in tow, matching my speed.

I smiled and started to laugh. "I mean, cupping vomit in my hand is never my idea of a good time." He gave me a sideways glance. "But everything is fine now."

"But I do need to find a bathroom as fast as humanly possible." I smiled. "And maybe a glass of wine."

"We can make that happen."

We corralled our children and suitcases through the train station in search of a bathroom…and hopefully some wine.

THIS IS NOT POSSIBLE

We made it to Barcelona relatively in one piece. Our apartment had a washer and dryer in the unit, so the first thing I did when we got there was unpack, soak the vomit-covered clothing from our train ride, shower, and start a load of laundry. I was utterly exhausted but beyond excited. Other than the night we spent there at the beginning of our trip, I had not been in Barcelona for eighteen years and even then I was only there for a couple of days. We planned to have a relaxing evening, getting acclimated to the new apartment/sleeping situation and walking to get some dinner. Our apartment for the week was across the street from one of Barcelona's most iconic and well-known sites--la

Sagrada Familia, Gaudi's historic cathedral and unique piece of art.

Seeing and touring the cathedral was a bucket list item for me. I had been wanting to come back for eighteen years to see its beauty and progress. The cathedral was infamous for its never-ending and outrageously ambitious construction. When I last visited, the inside was not complete and several of the current standing towers were merely an idea. I was taken aback by how much had changed.

Museums with small kiddos were not for the faint of heart. We had intentionally kept them at a minimum on this trip--only the most historic ones and only every few days, preceded and followed by lots of snacks, playtime outside at one of Spain's many playgrounds, and unstructured time wherever we were staying. For the most part, this served us exceptionally well, but I was anxious for the tour tomorrow. We walked to dinner and found a restaurant where we could sit outside with a clear view of the "familia" (the shortened name my five-year-old started to call it…it was love at first sight for him).

As soon as we sat down, I played up how cool it would be.

"Kiddos!" I waited until all three of my children were looking at me. And then, in a very dramatic, theatrical voice, I hollered, "Look at that!" I pointed to the glowing cathedral, spotlights illuminating its brilliance. They all looked towards it and, meeting my energy, let out excited, audible gasps.

"It's so beautiful, Mommy!"

"I love the familia!"

"That looks really cool."

I smiled and leaned deeper into the moment. "And guess what?"

"What?!"

"We get to go.." I paused for effect. "INSIDE. Tomorrow!"

They cheered, clapped and danced.

All right. Excitement built.

The next morning, when we arrived for our tour, the line to enter was at least thirty people deep. I saw the anxiety rising in my three-year-old daughter and five-year-old son. Both refused to walk and my husband and I took turns carrying them. Thankfully, my eight-year-old son needed no encouragement. In fact, he was in absolute awe of the building and rattled off incredibly thoughtful questions the whole way there--some I knew the answer to, many I didn't. We compiled a mental list of questions to find the answers to during the visit or afterwards. His curiosity was the best.

When we entered the cathedral, everywhere I looked was another spectacular detail---the sights, sounds, textures, and smells exhilarated me. Time momentarily stopped as I took it all in. Looking at my husband, I saw that he felt the same way.

A few seconds later, I was snapped back to reality. "Mommy. I'm hungry. I want a snack," my five-year-old said while grabbing my hand.

I was still holding my daughter and moved her from my left hip to my right to give the left side, getting more sore by the second, a break. I took my son's hand and said, "Not right now, buddy. We just had breakfast and food is not allowed in la familia."

"Hmph." My son was not pleased. My husband picked him up, in an attempt to calm him down. It worked momentarily.

I inched towards my husband, giving him a sideways hug, the children on our hips preventing a full embrace. "Pretty cool, huh?"

He looked around the space before his eyes met mine. "This place is incredible."

I glanced at our children and turned back to my husband. "Let's get a family picture while everyone is relatively in a good mood."

"Good call."

I managed to free my phone from my pocket and caught the eye of a kind stranger. I asked them, in Spanish, if they could take a picture of us. They nodded. I thanked them. When I got my phone back, I looked at the picture. My oldest had wandered out of the frame before it was taken, my daughter turned away from the camera and my middle son, who my husband put down for the picture, had his back fully to the camera and was reaching for me to pick him up. My eyes were closed.

I laughed and showed the picture to my husband. "Well, we tried."

He laughed. "We did."

We were there, together, and that's what really mattered.

We opted for a self-guided tour, making our way through the various spaces and reading the information posted throughout. I could have stayed there for hours, each thing more compelling than the next. My oldest continued to soak it all in. He was increasingly interested in history and we were basically standing in a history book. My younger two children, despite their excitement yesterday and this morning, were not having it. At all. I had been carrying either my three-year-old or my five-year-old the entire time. My arms were sore and the consistent frame of "are we done yet?" and "can I have a snack? I'm huuuungry!" was starting to take its toll on my patience.

My daughter was nearing the end of her road. We wandered to an outside exhibit to admire the building from a new angle and see the details of the architecture we had just read about inside. I thought the fresh air might have a calming effect on the tantrum I could see rising. In an attempt to better enjoy the view and give my arms a break, I momentarily put my daughter down. My arms felt like they might actually fall off.

Big mistake.

She instantly started cry-screaming. I took a few deep breaths, attempting to calm her down without picking her up.

She's okay. I'm okay. We're all okay.

She threw herself to the ground and screamed even louder.

Focus on the building and its beauty. She'll be okay. Let her feel her feelings. She'll work through them on her own time. It's better this way.

I crouched down to hug her and comfort her. "I'm here. Mommy's here. Look at the building. Keep breathing nice big breaths."

"I don't WANT to breathe, Mommy!"

"Let's stand up, silly girl!" I stayed positive and calm since any other approach might turn this meltdown into a blood curdling scream situation that I wanted to avoid.

A minute later, a young person working at the museum walked up to my mid-meltdown daughter and me. Her scrunched up face and annoyed eyes told me that this was quite possibly the last conversation she wanted to be having. She looked me straight in the eye, pointed to my daughter and said, in a subdued voice, "This is not possible."

I immediately picked my daughter up and started to bounce her, saying to the worker, under my breath in a very impatient tone. "Oh, it's possible. It's happening." Beads of sweat were now dripping from my forehead, back, arms and legs.

Who did she think she was? My daughter is three! Of course she is going to have a meltdown. She's not the only one. Kids should be allowed to be kids, even here.

I was livid. And embarrassed. I felt my mama bear tendencies boil up.

The woman looked at me without any expression before awkwardly walking back to her post, only a few feet away.

I turned to my husband, my face reddening with a growing frustration. "I fully realize that she should not be on the ground, but she IS only three."

He turned to me and gave me a kiss on my forehead. "I know, babe." He picked up our five-year-old, who was also on the verge of a meltdown. "I think it might be time to go."

I snorted. "Yes, I think you are right."

My eight-year-old, still gazing at the building and not noticing the meltdowns around him, pointed up. "Mom! Do you see that up there? Can you believe that people have been building this for so many years? And it's still not done!" He continued to share facts that he learned from our tour of the cathedral, barely stopping to breathe as he did.

I smiled. His curiosity and love for learning immediately slowed my heart rate and brought me back to the magical moment with my children at this special place. "I know, buddy. Isn't that so cool? There are so many incredible talented artists, architects, engineers and more that have worked on this building. It is so impressive." I paused, looking up. "And magical."

He nodded, eyes still gazing at the building. "It really is magical, Mom. It really is."

My husband and I gathered the children and headed to the exit, soaking in the beauty of the place one last time on our way out. We walked across the street to a playground to let our children burn some energy and give my husband and I some time to recover and prepare for the rest of the day. It was not even noon and I felt like I had experienced enough emotions to fill at least several days.

As I sat on a bench at the playground, I smiled. Despite the stress and sweat, the visit to the la Sagrada Familia was beyond worth it. I thought about what the women said to me- "this is not possible." I laughed.

Sure, going to a cathedral with three young children without incident was not, in fact, possible.

But you know what was possible? Going on an adventure across Spain with three small children.

It was possible.

It was magical.

It was the trip of a lifetime.

Meeting Mother India

Laurie Riedman

I didn't think any trip could live up to the phrase, *"it was a trip of a lifetime,"* until I traveled halfway around the globe to visit our daughter. Almost twenty years later, that trip continues to impact my life.

My husband Rich and I had finally settled into our tiny cube of a hotel room after our 15-hour fight, bleary-eyed, stunned, and simultaneously exhausted and wired. We had only been in Mumbai less than 90 minutes and had already been pickpocketed. We no longer had Rich's credit card, American cash, or Indian Rupees. Upon calling our credit card company, we discovered that my card was associated with his – so my card would no longer work either.

Ok, India. We've arrived.

Thankfully, the hotel was pre-paid, as was our driver, who was due to pick us up the following day to take us on the 4-hour drive to Pune to meet up with our eldest daughter, Liz.

Liz surprised us a year ago by declaring India her study-abroad destination. Before we knew it, she was boarding the plane to Pune, India, at the start of her junior year.

Liz had been living with her Indian host family for the past three months. With her stay soon to end, we had decided to visit and travel with her for three weeks and bring her home with us. Once the dates, plane tickets, and 20-day itinerary were set, we had done all the necessary preparations, including multiple vaccinations, visa applications, and acquired travel gear. We sprayed our clothing with a strong insect repellent at the urging of a malaria travel advisory. Finally, we thought we were prepared.

We weren't.

It was advice Liz had hastily given me during an unstable internet phone call a few weeks before our departure that would significantly impact our trip—and, consequently, my life.

"Mom, you must leave your Western viewpoint at home," Liz said thoughtfully but calmly. "You and Dad have to do whatever you can to let go of all your expectations for how things should go. India is like no other place you've been," she cautioned. "I've learned that as Westerners, we must meet Mother India where she is. If you can do that – you will have a better experience."

I trusted Liz knew what she was talking about because she had done this herself in the past few months. While she had seen the wonders of the Kerola rivers from the deck of a houseboat and celebrated many festivals, including the colorful Holi, she had quite a few terrifying ones too, including boarding the wrong bus and not realizing it until being dropped off in the middle of the night in a village hours from where she was supposed to be and experiencing sexual harassment among crowded streets. She also had supported a fellow American student suffering PTSD from unwelcome sexual groping by a group of older men.

During our three weeks of travel, many moments tested us to take off our "Western eyeglasses" and see Mother India for who she was.

It had been hours in the car while our driver navigated windy roads and dusty paths, narrowly passing trucks, tuk-tuks, and buses so overloaded it was a miracle they didn't topple over. Unfortunately, we were stuck in a traffic jam, most likely caused by an animal stubbornly standing in the road or construction closing the road for an undetermined amount of time with no warning.

Sitting in the back of the car with Rich and Liz, I was frantically fanning myself with the guidebook, hoping this "flowing air" would alleviate how hot and sticky I felt. Unfortunately, the car "AC" we had paid extra for blew air far from cool.

Sweat dripping down my back, I opened the window despite knowing from experience that the loud city sounds would no longer be muted and dirt from the road was sure to stick to the sweat on my skin, making the "sponge bath" I'd be taking later that night more of a challenge.

Looking out the window, I took in our surroundings. Dozens of people stood or sat along the road, trying to find any spot in the light shade. It was then that I noticed them.

A family of four sitting on the ground under thinly laced shade from a bare-branched tree. I watched them -- first, noticing their thread-bare clothing, dirty hands, and feet. Then, I felt pity for them -- instantly judging how hard and awful their life must be. I imagined they were probably living in the squalor of the slums we had just passed.

My mind recalled our dinner conversation last night.

While enjoying a delicious dinner at an open-air restaurant on the banks of a lake, Rich and I agreed that we had never seen this level of poverty. Between bites of colorful and delightful curries and saffron rice, we recalled the massive slums we'd seen smack-dab in the city center, often directly under shadows of expensive high-rise apartments and billboards advertising Gucci and Rolex. We had seen slum after slum – miles and miles of tiny makeshift homes fashioned with corrugated cardboard or misshapen tin sheets on top of one another in a jumble. As we shared what a shame it was, it wasn't lost on me that I was experiencing what I had often read about—the chasm between the system of social hierarchy of Indian castes and tourists like us.

I recalled what we had seen sharing our insights and feelings as we sat comfortably at our table, tiny twinkling lights strung above us, the lake beside us, as an impeccably dressed waiter served us course after course.

I returned to the present moment, waiting in that traffic jam, looking at this family; at that moment, I saw something different.

The family I watched was having a picnic of sorts thanks to a nearby paanwalas, a vendor selling paan, a popular Indian snack made with nuts, raisins, dried fruit, and spices wrapped in betel leaves.

The family appeared to be sharing one single leaf. Could this be their only meal of the day?

The couple looked no older than Liz. The father, thin-faced with a smile revealing crooked yellow teeth, sat alongside the woman I assumed was his wife. Her hair, jet black, was pulled back in a braid. She wore what once was a brightly colored sari - now a bit muted and dusty - a traditional gold ring on her nose among numerous thin gold bracelets lining her arm. A toddler, running around them, barefoot and laughing, occasionally stopped to draw in the dirt with a stick. An infant, scrawny legs outstretched, was held close to her chest. I watched as the man held the leaf to the child, who stopped long enough to take a quick nibble. Then, smiling, he reached over to his wife, gently pushing a stray strand of her long dark hair off her sweaty face, allowing her to take a bite. The look they exchanged was one of pure love and happiness.

Hello, Mother India.

Later that week, our driver took us to a hilltop, popular with the locals, at sunset. He was so excited to show us what he promised would be the most beautiful sunset we'd ever seen. We would soon learn that you need to be in the present moment to appreciate Indian sunsets because they don't last long. You've got to catch them at just the right moment due to the short viewing "window." You'd watch for the setting golden circle to show itself within a thin slice of the skyline sandwiched between the clouds above and the thick smog emanating from the city below. Start to finish; it took less than 3 minutes.

Other families arrived to enjoy the sunset and cool night air. While waiting with them, we sat on a stone wall at the top of a hill, looking at yet another slum in the valley below.

It was then that it happened again. I zeroed in on some movement below on the rooftops of those tiny unstable shacks that fit together like jigsaw puzzle pieces.

It was as if I was watching a movie - my eyes (the camera) took in the expanse of the entire panoramic scene below. Then, I slowly zoomed in to focus on one little section, allowing me a glimpse of an intimate moment amid that massive scene.

Lifting my 35mm camera so I could use my telephoto lens to zoom in on the movement I had just noticed, I focused in and saw a dozen or so children passing something to each other. Upon closer inspection, I saw what appeared to be an empty potato chip bag tied to a string. My goodness, those clever kids had fashioned their own kite! I watched them pass it to each other as they ran rooftop to rooftop – the sky slowly dimming behind them, making them dance in the shadows. The delight I saw through the lens was contagious. I felt their giddiness and happiness. They were kids being kids. I smiled on the inside.

Nice to meet you, Mother India.

On one of our last days, we were riding a tuk-tuk, an odd-looking contraption resembling a kaleidoscope on wheels. Each tuk-tuk is a unique expression of its owner's personality and creativity, painted in bright colors, decorated with patterns and fabrics, and flourishes.

A small bubble-like metal canopy shelters you from the sun and rain. The sides are open to the air, and you slide in behind the driver, perched at the helm – one hand on the small steering wheel and the other on the horn. Once you've agreed upon the destination and haggled on a price, off you go – zipping and zagging in and out of traffic with a mix of skill and courage. Tuk-tuk drivers are skilled at deftly maneuvering among an endless sea of other tuk-tuks, bicycles, cars, overflowing trucks, and people walking. Besides hearing the shouts of roadside vendors and honks of other drivers saying "I am here" or "Go ahead" with their horns. Tuk-Tuk engines make an annoying constant sound like a sick moped struggling at its highest gear. We whiz among the hustle and bustle of the city while our driver constantly pushes our distinctive horn toot-toooooooooooots, sounding like angry buzzing bees seeking nectar.

If there is a sound I associate with India, it is the never-ending succession of horns honking. There are so many horns! Each has its own tone, colliding with the sound of loudly sputtering motors and people yelling, selling their wares, and seeking our attention. Everyone is in a crushing rush. Tuk-tuk drivers are no exception because the faster they move, the more money they make.

Due to India's large, diverse population, many religions are observed – Hindu, Buddhist, Catholic, and Islam –to name a few. As a result, I experienced amazing religious tolerance as people observed and practiced their religions daily on top of one another.

On this trip to the market, our tuk-tuk driver, without any word or excuse for the delay, pulled over at what appeared to be a statue of some sort. He quickly exited and offered a marigold blossom he had grabbed from the colorful collection decorating his dashboard, bowed quickly, offered the flower to the statue, muttered a quick prayer or blessing, and just as promptly hopped back in, and we were on our way. During our trip, I witnessed Hindu ceremonies, the lovely call to prayer from an Islamic temple, as well as the familiar sound of the bells of a catholic church, all within a small space in a short amount of time. Everyone honors their beliefs without judgment, not just one day a week. It seemed these people lived their beliefs every day. This was refreshing. And so lovely to bear witness.

I see you, Mother India. I see you

I carry the lesson Liz encouraged me to learn on that trip every day. My time in India became the training wheels for my everyday mindfulness and meditation practice. Being able to "meet Mother India where she was" allowed me to witness the love, joy, beauty, and happiness she had to offer. Had I not let go of my Western expectations and allowed myself to zero in on so many mini-miracles - I would have missed the real India. I may have returned like others, only to say they would never return. I would have come back only with stories of poverty, beggars, no personal space, noise, air pollution, sexism, and so much more.

Nothing is all dark or all light. We can choose what to notice and what to let go of. This can be the difference between sadness and joy and love and hate.

Without slowing things down so we can notice, we miss lovely moments every day. I am so happy that I met Mother India at that point in my life. She allowed me to learn how to look past my judgments and Western views and to see—and experience—what mattered. I saw her people living their lives as best they could, finding happiness and joy no matter what their day brought or lacked.

This is the foundation upon which I've built my mindfulness practice, allowing me to meet my life where it is, let go of the tendency to judge myself and others, connect, and practice kindness and compassion. My life is better when I focus on what is happening now rather than worrying about the future or getting caught up in the past. *Thank you, Mother India. Thank you.*

Musings from 36,000 Feet

Ellen Newman

DATELINE: February 1, 2024, from Nairobi to San Francisco

Travel days are annoying, pesky and magical. Crazy long (29-hour) travel days create their own kind of liminal space. You are neither here nor there. Time is altered. You have dinner for breakfast or breakfast for dinner. The cabin crew alters reality by altering light, all according to schedule. When the two cities are 12 hours apart, life is upside down. But at least you don't have to reset your watch when you arrive!

Travel days begin with a flurry of activity: packing, organizing, making sure documents are handy. We all have a dossier, a record, that follows us wherever we go. Our passports and our faces are scanned. Leaving Nairobi after a fabulous ten days on safari, we were instructed to get out of the car so we could walk through a scanner at the side of the road. Only then was the driver allowed to drop us off at the entrance to the airport. In Dubai, we had a security check at our transfer gate, then again just before boarding the flight home. That last one, after a five-hour flight and four-hour layover, included a physical wanding for explosive powder and a search of our carry-on bags. I've never experienced that before. I was told it was at the request of the U.S. government. Better safe than sorry.

That's where I met the "tea lady," just two people ahead of me in line. Bold white letters on the back of her black T-shirt asked, "What am I wearing?" Any place besides a security line that would have been a conversation starter. When she finally turned around to retrieve her bags, I saw the words, "A *T-E-A* shirt," surrounding an image of a steaming cup of tea. I burst out laughing, a bit nervous with all the agents nearby. Pokerfaced as always, they ignored my giggles as they continued fumbling though our bags. Performance or necessity? Who knows. But later, on the plane, I connected with a world traveler and motivational speaker, originally from Kolkata but now from Colorado Springs, with a welcome sense of humor.

Airports are a universe unto themselves, both alike and unique. Who designs them? Who understands how they function? So many people are necessary to make the worldwide system work. Security workers in

Germany went on strike the day we left Nairobi, putting a major crimp in the system of international hubs and transfer points. How many people missed their connections that day? How many canceled flights had to be rebooked? Our Canadian-based safari leader was rebooked from Nairobi to Cairo to Warsaw and then on to her home in Toronto. Exhausting! The whole complex system fascinates me.

So does people-watching in the airport. Early morning (between 4 and 8 am) in Dubai, we saw mostly westerners and South Asians waiting to transfer to their second or third flights on journeys that condense the world into an ever more connected place. Later Emiratis or Saudis, the men in long white shirts called thawbs and women in black abayas, began arriving for their flights. Their black and white stood out against the sea of denim most passengers were wearing, giving the effect of teams of penguins racing for their flights.

In Nairobi we encountered a large family ahead of us on the security line: an older woman, two moms with babies wrapped on their backs, younger kids, and a teen girl as gangly as a giraffe trying to gracefully pry off her pink high-top sneaks and put them into the bin.

Each family member awkwardly carried a heavy coat as if it were an alien object. A younger teen boy, the only English speaker in the group, explained that they were from the Congo on their way to Georgia in the U.S. That's when I noticed they were carrying white bags with a UN refugee assistance logo. When we arrived in Dubai, two representatives from the agency, clipboards in hand, waited by the gate to assist them on to the next leg of their journey.

I got shivers thinking about this family from the Congo coming to America. Of course, I have no idea what they were fleeing. Coming from the Congo, with no adult males in the group, one could only guess. Recent civil unrest, crime, terrorism and armed conflict have displaced more than seven million people. This was just one family.

Watching them deal with airport rituals, so familiar to those of us who travel for business or pleasure, reminded me that most of us travel as part of a roundtrip from home and back again. Most likely, they were on a one-way passage connecting the world they knew to an entirely different one. Their travel day was just the beginning of the *NEW*. Learning a new language will be an adjustment. Finding jobs. Going to school. Becoming American will take a lifetime.

From our cocoon 36,000 feet above the earth, I was excited for this family seeking a brighter, safer future.

They connected me to my grandparents, all four of whom made similar journeys by ship more than a hundred years ago. I was imagining possibilities for the two babies on their mothers' backs, for the boy who was their intermediary to the western world and for the gangly girl in her pink high tops.

Welcome to your future. May it be as bright as your expectations and as easy as an Emirates flight.

Patria or Homeland

Jackie Alcalde Marr

The turquoise and teal
of the magic Mediterranean.
Or the blues and grey-green
of the promising Pacific.
Both shouldered the ships,
both tumble in and lay white foam on the sand.

Rolling hills with rows of stitching,
olive trees with branches swaying.
Or rolling hills with rows of stitching,
grapevines heavy with indigo and sun.
Both give their fruit for family and friends
around the table, long into the night.

The bold black bull
on the stark slope.
Or the burley brown bear
roaring from the forest.
Both carry the strength of wills
and the wants and the wisdom.

The wide brim of the Cordobés,

flat and fierce, finery from the south.

Or the upturned edges of the ten-gallon,

covering the crown of the cowboy

Both adorn the courageous beast

atop a more courageous beast, hooves stirring the earth.

Tongue between the teeth,

says stature and schooling.

Or the tongue on the roof,

its soft hiss says ships have sailed and stopped.

Both from the same ancient roots,

eloquence spilling from their lips, creating change.

Spain or States,

Patria or Homeland.

Both live in the blood and the bones,

in the heart and the soul

Both thread their identity through generations,

those who left and those who stayed.

Both are home.

BIOGRAPHIES

Jackie Alcalde Marr

I am becoming a person who does the things that make me happy, who makes the time to nurture old friendships, and who gives myself space to focus some energy on my own wellbeing and the wellbeing of those in my orbit. Becoming.

I think we're all in a process of becoming more and more of all the aspects of our full selves. In years past, I had become a singer and amateur guitar player. I had become a business professional who spent a few years in banking and insurance, then nestled into a long career in leadership and organization development at global, high-tech companies. I had become a stereotypical road-warrior consultant, as well as a lucky ex-pat, living just outside of England. I had become a leader of many teams and a Director of Organization & Talent Development at Oracle Corporation.

I've become an entrepreneur, a certified leadership and life coach, an independent consultant and educator, a co-author of Social Media At Work: How Social Networking Propels Organizational Performance, and a certified book coach. I've become an aspiring author of historical fiction, passionate about honoring my ancestors with the stories of their immigration from Spain through Hawaii and on to their American lives in the Bay Area of California.

I've always been decidedly a dog person, a lover of all things coffee-flavored, one who chooses mountains a little more often than the ocean, and definitely a red over white wine lover (the bigger and bolder, the better!)

Alas, I wish I'd become a better wife to my husband, a more loving friend, a super-fit sixty-two-year-old, and a proud veteran of the Camino de Santiago. But I'm still becoming, so I look forward to all of that around the bend!

Katherine Cartwright

I think. I observe. I reflect. I notice. I watch. I listen. It all goes into the cauldron of my imagining and, when it's ready, I pour it onto the page and see what its become. I explore wild landscapes -- on the land and in the soul. I explore the landscapes of poetry, myth, and the fractured-expanding-healing self. Our soul's landscape is littered with stories that tell us something about ourselves. We don't even have to dig down deep to find them, but they can take us deep. Writing opens a landscape into my own human experience and I hope to connect with others in theirs. When I was little, I wanted to be a fossil hunter. I loved looking for the stories in the stone. That may be part of why I love poetry. I can hold up a moment and suspend it in timeless reflection.

Putting words together brushes away the dust and soil to reveal what lies beneath, what once lived and now lives differently. A colleague once said this after reading my work, "Few things happen in this world without leaving traces, whether they be physical or metaphysical, but few people spend much time looking for those signs and asking what they might mean."

I earned a degree in Journalism from Indiana University, where I also studied creative writing and literature, and a Master of Divinity from the Lutheran Theological Seminary at Gettysburg. I work with congregations in transition, helping them to find a way between their past and present, so they can bring awareness and choice to who they are becoming. I develop and lead workshops, including *Anthropology for the Soul: Unearthing Story for Healing, Growth, and Transformation* and *Thirteen Moons: Tracking the Wild Mare.* My poetry collection, *Claws of Uthurunku*, was released in 2019. My home is in Bucks County, Pennsylvania, along the beautiful Delaware River.

My blog, *Awakened Spirit,* and author page on Facebook:

http://kateknodel.blogspot.com

https://www.facebook.com/profile.php?id=100062494672014

Wendy Coad

I'm an artist through and through. I picked up a brush long before I ever picked up a pen. But life has a way of throwing you into the deep end. At 17, I walked out the door and never looked back, and at 19, I was hitchhiking around the world with my sister. I didn't follow the rules—art school, education, then another art degree—moving, creating, singing in a cappella group with friends, showing my work in the city. I landed in New York, where I embraced the wild, messy beauty of the holistic scene, learning and teaching what I practiced, living a life that was always on the edge.

In the 25 years that I lived there, New York gave me a lot—love, loss, and the grit to keep going. I had long-duration artist residencies at PS1 and then another one in Miami Beach after I moved there. In the meantime, I looked after my mum before she passed and then my in-laws.

Then the pandemic hit hard, and the world stopped. But out of the darkness came this fierce, amazing Sisterhood. In those two years, I turned inward, painting thousands of artworks, writing over 100,000 words, and crafting my memoir. They saved me and held me up, and now I'm forever connected to them and to the work we did together. I write like I paint—with passion, in broad, messy strokes. It's all because of the Sisterhood, those badass women. That's the real story and why I'm here today.

Maggie Croushore

Ever since I was a child, I have identified as a nurturer; it is within my nature to care for others. My mom loves to tell the stories of me from preschool where my teachers nicknamed me "Mother Maggie." I was always taking care of the other kids, tucking them into their covers for naptime, giving them hugs when they were sad, and 'helping' out the teachers in any way that I could.

While obviously fuzzy, my memories from my earliest years center around this theme of nurturing others. From "teaching" a staircase full of astute stuffed animals in my basement to being the self-proclaimed "hugger" during sibling video game sessions, my role was taking care of others.

When I became a mother myself, my whole world changed. The concept of mothering was no longer a piece of my nature, it was my number one role. I had a beautiful human in front of me (or on me in most cases those first many, many months), and my protective mama bear nature kicked into high gear. I felt a deeper sense of purpose to create a world, locally and globally, that was better not only for my child but for every child. This renewed sense of purpose was motivating, if not overwhelming at times. It only intensified with the birth of all three of my children.

I carry this mama bear mentality to the things I care about most. An advocate for educational and health equity, I have dedicated myself to creating opportunities for children. I started my career as a middle school teacher and was a founding member of an ambitious Cradle to Career program in a major city, where I helped scale from (quite literally) two people in a windowless room at City Hall to a sustainably-funded, multi-faceted program serving youth and families across the city. While rewarding, this work can be exhausting. After one particularly stressful day of working and mothering, I opened a Google Doc and started writing. Journaling quickly became a part of my daily routine and a source of healing, joy, hope, and love. Writing was, and remains, a saving grace.

I believe in the power of storytelling to create individual and societal change. In my "free" time, I write, run, cook, bake, and explore the Twin Cities with my husband, adorable three young children, and energetic corgi.

You can find my newsletter, All or Something, on Substack.

https://maggiefordcroushore.substack.com/.

Amber Field

Amber Field is a Lecturer at the University of Wisconsin-Madison and author of the new book, *Agile Discovery & Delivery: A Survival Guide for New Software Engineers & Tech Entrepreneurs.* She has been an executive leader in tech, agile proponent, and engineer for her entire career at a number of organizations including IBM, National Geographic, Oracle Utilities (formerly Opower), Capital One, and Singlewire Software. Amber frequently speaks at conferences and blogs at amberrfield.com. She lives in Madison, WI with her husband, Graham, four kids, and two cats.

Sandra Holy

Sandra Holy was born in Montreal, Quebec, and hitch-hiked to the West Coast in her late teens. There, she met an adventurer with whom she climbed mountains and travelled to distant places. A home, a marriage and young family later, she left the home and marriage behind and began a new adventure with her children. After a foray into public speaking, she obtained a BA in Communications, a Certificate in Family Studies and worked as a Regional Communications Consultant for the federal government.

A major life transition became the catalyst for a new journey of healing and self-enquiry. As a natural development of this journey, Sandra became a practitioner of an integrative process that incorporates electro-magnetic field work, intention and self-awareness practices. She has taken courses across North America to advance her training and uses this work to support people in living a more joyful, empowered and authentic life.

Sandra enjoys observing people and has been writing, in one form or another, for most of her life. In recent years she has been crafting her book, "The Singing Bird: A Memoir About the Hidden Story of My Life." This is her first major work.

Sandra has two amazing children and lives in British Columbia, Canada with a Norfolk Pine named Guinevere and a coffee tree named Mocha: the thirstiest plant in the house.

Ariadne Horstman, CFP®, RLP®

Ariadne founded Appreciate Finance in 2015 and merged her business with Tamarind Financial Planning in 2022.

Her goals are to help individuals and families realize personal goals and dreams through comprehensive financial planning and investment management. She has practiced as a CFP® since 2008, advising families and individuals. Prior to that, she worked in the tech industry in Silicon Valley after a career in consulting and conference production in France.

She is a Registered Life Planner® with the Kinder Institute, practicing life planning with clients to ensure their finances are fully supportive of their objectives as they move toward realizing them. Having lived in France, India and the UK, she has international skills to bring to those with cross border situations.

Ariadne is based in Palo Alto with her husband and also spends time at other locations such as Oxford, UK. They are now empty nesters, as their two children pursue studies.

A graduate of Smith College, she completed her financial planning coursework at UC Santa Cruz. She loves the outdoors, yoga, Pilates, reading, creative writing and meditation.

Katharina Hren

I started writing when I was young as a way to cope with loneliness and survive my parents' divorce due to my father's alcoholism. Because of my love for learning, I spent far too many years in academia, first via a master's degree in Foreign Language and Literature and then a master's degree in Community Psychology, but it was becoming a yoga teacher that helped me to finally heal. I now work as a trauma therapist and mindfulness/yoga teacher in Milwaukee, WI, where I live with my son, Gustav and my partner, Steve. I am currently writing a memoir about my passion for travel, living in three countries before the age of 4, single parenting, and healing from generational trauma.

Ellen Newman

It all started in Jakarta. I was half a world away from home and loving every minute of every day. I met new people, explored new places, tasted new food and shopped for treasures I never knew existed. I tingled with life. Everything I encountered for six months was fresh and new. Even the ghosts. Yes, the ghosts. The ancient explorers. The traders who sailed the monsoons to collect pepper for the emperor. The colonial governors and their dangerous dungeons.

My six-month adventure in Indonesia, courtesy of my husband's surprise USAID legal assignment in Southeast Asia, fed my travel bug and led to my travel writing and photography. Pieces I wrote on that journey appeared in the *Dallas Morning News*, *Honolulu Advertiser* and *Vancouver Sun*.

Back home in San Francisco, where I had a long career in nonprofit public relations, the internet beckoned. In 2017, it became the venue for my new venture, Hidden-inSite.com, an online travel and photo magazine. Hidden-inSite explores overlooked places, secret spots that surprise and delight. It takes nuanced and lively looks at locales famous and familiar. Hidden-InSite is the answer to the question, what's around the bend or hidden inside the cathedral.

Those ghosts? They pop up from time to time, reminding me to look between the layers, to picture life in different times and places. Those ghosts oblige me to notice what is and what was. They guide me to explore the world with imagination, curiosity and heart.

T-Ann Pierce

T-Ann Pierce is a life, confidence, and parenting coach and writer with a background in Personal and Family Development. With heartfelt candor and humor, T-Ann captures truths and offers real-world solutions to the conundrum of being human. She is a mother to four grown kids and a grandmother to one yummy little girl. She and her husband live north of Chicago, recently downsized, and are trying to figure out what to eat for dinner.

Laurie Riedman

Laurie Riedman is a personal and relationship coach, writer, and storyteller. After thirty-five years running her own PR and marketing firm, she transitioned her consulting to coaching, founding b.u. coaching to support those—like her—who seek to embrace their truths and be their best selves in all aspects of their personal and professional lives.

Writing and publishing essays on her Substack blog, More Than Words, and her memoir Diamonds in the Dirt: Stories From a Junkyard Girl are part of her healing journey. She has also published essays in Bluff and Vine. Her writing is included in several anthologies, including Volume I and II of Badass Sisterhood, which she co-edited with Susan Walter, and the *Sensual Soul*

Shine anthology, published by Unbound Press in July 2024.

Laurie lives, writes, and coaches from her home along Canandaigua Lake in the Finger Lakes of New York. Married to her life partner Rich for over thirty-eight years, they have founded three successful companies and raised three amazing daughters: Liz, Beck, and Hannah.

She and Susan Walter co-founded Badass Sisterhood Publishing and published the two Badass Sisterhood anthologies to encourage and support other women in their writing and publishing journeys.

Check out Laurie's blog and books and contact her at www.laurieriedman.com.

Terri Tomoff

My husband Bill likes to say I live life by trying to stick 10 lbs of stuff in a five lb. bag quite faithfully. It's been that way for me for six decades, and for the most part, it has served me well as I quilt, write, travel, referee soccer, and seek adventure around every corner. As the owner of NeedleOnFull, a successful Tshirt Quilt and Long Arming business, I help my clients preserve their most precious memories with a treasured keepsake.

Adding value to my life and others by being the best wife, mother, sister, friend, chief caregiver, and hope provider brings me joy. Over the past 25+ years, I have advocated for childhood cancer awareness using gratitude, grit, and love. My 28-year-old son, Ryan, is a 5X cancer survivor, and his sister, Olivia, is a 31-year-old sibling of a survivor. In those years spent in and out of hospitals, I learned I could only control record keeping and taking thousands of photos to write a book about our family's experiences someday.

In 2012 I began a daily blog, which helped me fall in love with writing. Ten years later, daily writing helped catapult me to write and publish, *The Focused Fight: A Childhood Cancer Journey From Mayhem to Miracles* in 2021. It is a heartfelt recount from the original diagnosis of Leukemia (ALL) to where we stand today - culminating with a deeper appreciation for the "little things in life, the power of a chocolate chip cookie, or a handwritten note."

To learn more about me (and when my sophomore book will be published):

Website https://www.territomoff.com/

FB: https://www.facebook.com/territomoff/

LI: https://www.linkedin.com/in/territomoff/

Susan Walter

I'm a Special Care planner, educator and Chartered Special Needs Consultant for families with a disability focused on the needs of today and tomorrow by integrating financial, legal, and benefits resource planning. It's not my first rodeo -I learned firsthand from the school of life about navigating the systems of healthcare, social services, education, law, and finance to create the best possible quality-of-life future for my adult child who has impactful Epilepsy.

I share this journey through writing, consulting, and wealth management with the hope that my intrepid, indomitable spirit and humorous approach to life and parenting a child with a health disability helps others feel better about their own life moments, especially the mishaps! I'm writing a memoir recounting life with epilepsy, recounting the macro and micro moments dealing with the unplanned challenges no one could prepare me for.

Writing helps me to loosen my grip to let life unfold in its majestic, sometimes arduous, bounty. Virginia Woolf wrote, "Arrange the pieces as they come." It's a reminder, an action, a philosophy, and my model for getting through the tough times…after all is said and done, I want my family to look forward to spending time with me through all of life's adventures. I say "Yes" to travel, trail runs, experiments in the kitchen, and adventure.

I live with Bill, my patient husband of 30+ years and partner in problem-solving; and Henry, our adult son and his seizure response service dog, Grayson, a golden retriever love-muffin. Our daughter, Eleanor, and her partner, Will, visit often with their dogs, Lousie and Finn.

Acknowledgements:

Thank you to whoever oversees it all ...of orchestrating the ups and downs of our lives... the good stuff, the bad stuff, and the stuff in between that inspire writers to write. We all have a story, and there is so much power in sharing our stories.

This book would not be possible without Writing in Community (WIC). Back in 2019, when our worlds narrowed to the brady-bunch Zoom boxes on our computer screens - WIC brought us together and helped us birth Badass Sisterhood - a community of amazing creative women who are not afraid to share their truth as words on a page.

After a few years of writing on WIC, the original ten writers decided to create our first Anthology so many of us could call ourselves "published" authors for the first time!

We are grateful we found and supported each other as we strengthened our voices and writing craft, unleashing our creativity.

Since our first Badass Sisterhood Anthology was published in 2023, we've added a few more badass sisters to the collective, and this second edition is the result of our exploration of the topics of roots and wings or home and travel.

We thank our badass sisters for trusting us to publish their words. We are expanding our "grand experiment in publishing" by making this book available on Amazon.

To Ellen Newman, one of our original writers, we appreciate your assistance and expertise in photo editing. And to Wendy Coad, another of the original badass sisters, we are grateful for your creative spirit in sharing your artwork again for our cover.

Lastly, we appreciate all the fabulous humans who inspire our stories and words. Without your support, this project certainly wouldn't be possible. And we thank you, our readers, for supporting our passion by reading our words.

We agree with the wise Ben Franklin, who said, *"Either write something worth reading or do something worth writing."* In other words, be badass!

Laurie Riedman & Susan Walter
Badassery Co-Editors

Manufactured by Amazon.ca
Acheson, AB